MICHAEL LEACH has been a professional wildlife photographer and author since 1977. He has written fifteen books and his photographs have been published in countless magazines and books in over sixty countries. He has filmed wildlife programmes for both ITV and BBC. Michael is in great demand on the professional lecture circuit and has been described as a 'unique wildlife humorist'. He lives with his family in Shropshire.

Michael Leach

HIDDEN SHALLOWS

Confessions of a
Wildlife Photographer

Quandary
Press

Published by
Quandary Press, Brookside, Kinnerley
Oswestry, Shropshire
SY10 8DB

ISBN 0-9540431-0-3

Designed and typeset by
John Neilson, Llansilin, Oswestry
Set in Adobe Garamond

Line drawings by Keith Offord

All photographs by Michael Leach
except photograph of author on back cover by Dave Shaw

Printed and bound in Great Britain by Biddles Ltd.
www.biddles.co.uk

Contents

Foreword

For some wholly inexplicable reason wildlife photography seems to be regarded as an exciting and interesting profession. But, as in so many other careers, outsiders only ever see the good bits. Parts of my job are truly wonderful: I have the time and opportunity to sit and watch some of the world's most fascinating animals. But to get to this position takes planning, luck, discomfort and a generous portion of devious skullduggery. These are all essential elements that allow wildlife photographers to do their job, but no-one ever notices this background work: these are the Hidden Shallows.

I

A Dead-End Job

When I first set out to become a wildlife photographer, it was a very calculated decision. I wanted to work with animals but tame, cute creatures were not at all appealing. Scrubbed, antiseptic veterinary surgeries or the daily chore of milking two hundred cows held no allure for me. I didn't remotely fancy the idea of treating cats with scabby ears or delivering breached lambs at three o'clock in the morning. No, wild animals were the only possible vocation; work should be fun. I wanted to set up my tent in remote places that were miles from the beaten track. It seemed the only sensible occupation for anyone. But at the age of eighteen I had absolutely no idea of how the commercial world worked and soon discovered that there were very few jobs that paid people to stand out in woods and mountains to watch wildlife.

Like almost everyone else I first became interested in wildlife through TV programmes, books and magazines. It suddenly occurred to me that someone must provide photographs for the books that had fascinated me for so many years. Even in my naivety it was obvious that wildlife photography involved travelling to remote and exciting lands. I can still remember the thrill of this revelation. It was as if a light had been switched on – at last here was my ideal career. I immediately launched into a string of detailed daydreams, fantasies set in the near future when I was paid to track down gorillas and wolves, battling against the elements to produce films of phenomena never seen before.

So with encouraging words from my careers teacher still ringing in my ears, 'You're mad, absolutely crazy. No-one can possibly make a living like this. Do something sensible, become an accountant. Keep animals as a hobby. You'll starve', I launched myself enthusiastically into the unknown.

Today I understand that no-one's dreams are fulfilled easily but when I hit the first hurdle all those years ago it was unexpected and overwhelming. Wildlife photography as a career, like most creative fields, has a built-in paradox. Publishers will not use your work until you become known – and you cannot become known until someone publishes your work. Before earning any money I had to build up a collection of worthwhile pictures to show publishers, in the hope that they would be impressed and offer me lucrative contracts. Ideally my pictures should show species that had never before been photographed. Almost every British animal had been photographed *ad nauseam*: the world's most elusive animals all lived in locations far more exotic than Shropshire.

But expeditions required money and I had none at all. My early projects were much more modest and required no expensive air tickets. I spent my first professional summer studying and photographing hedgehogs. In this case the word 'professional' is used in the abstract. Although wildlife photography was my occupation, it was producing no cash at all – not a single penny. But at parties at least it allowed me to say coolly,

'Well actually I'm a professional wildlife photographer'.

In more practical terms, although this was not the perfect start to the exotic future I had in mind, at least hedgehogs cost nothing and lived in my parents' back garden, which kept travelling expenses to a bare minimum. I worked mainly with wild animals but also kept a tame hedgehog for a while to photograph some of the more secretive and tricky behaviour sequences.

To keep body and soul together I took a part-time job, serving petrol at a local service station, starting at six o'clock in the morning and finishing at lunchtime. This paid for film and fitted in perfectly with the activities of my nocturnal subjects. Hedgehogs were far removed from the gorillas of my dreams but at least they were wild animals and for three months they ruled my existence; I lived and breathed hedgehogs. But I am only flesh and blood and eventually even hedgehogs lost their charm. The project ended and I moved on to study foxes. But the hedgehogs were to return to haunt me.

One sunny Friday afternoon in November the telephone rang: it was a researcher from the BBC in London. This was my first contact with a television company and I was desperate to please.

'My name is Ralph, we're working on a programme that shows how animals survive the winter. I hear you're an expert on hedgehogs and have some kind of breeding colony there; you couldn't bring down one of your hibernating hedgehogs to the studio, could you?'

The world of wildlife professionals is relatively small, and so news travels around quickly. I vaguely knew other people in the field and on the rare occasions we met, problems and experiences were swapped and then the stories got passed around. The BBC has an excellent intelligence network, they can usually find what they need quickly and efficiently but this time the normally reliable grapevine had developed a fault and slightly distorted the reality of my work.

The closest I had ever got to a breeding colony of hedgehogs was to photograph a pregnant female called Rosie, who had last been seen disappearing under a blackthorn hedge about four months earlier. She was presumably tucked up somewhere fast asleep. But this was the BBC and I had absolutely no intention of turning them away; it was too good an opportunity.

'It's a bit too warm here at the moment,' I carefully explained, 'the hedgehogs are getting sleepy but haven't quite gone into full hibernation yet. When do you need one?'

'The programme goes out next Thursday; is there any chance they'll be asleep by then?' enquired Ralph. 'Oh and by the way, the BBC does have a budget for these things. If you can supply a hedgehog and bring it down to the studio, we'll pay you a fee of course, and travelling expenses.'

The smooth talking Ralph certainly had the knack of constructing a well-reasoned and powerful argument. This was the first time ever that someone from the media world had said 'we'll pay you' to me. I was completely broke and wildly keen to enter the inner circle. I just couldn't resist.

'Well, the forecasters say the temperature will drop at the weekend; if they're right, the hedgehogs will be out cold by Thursday,' I told him casually.

We left it there and I promised to contact Ralph as soon as my hedgehogs went to sleep.

That evening was spent telephoning everyone who had ever expressed even the remotest interest in hedgehogs. Surely someone would have one tucked away in their compost heap or behind the garden shed? There was a terrible inevitability about their answers: hedgehogs seemed to have vanished from the face of the earth. It was almost as if they had become extinct overnight. No one had seen even a wide-awake hedgehog for weeks, let alone knew of a hibernating animal. After three hours of fruitless searching I was forced to abandon the quest. BBC researchers rarely work at weekends; Ralph would have to wait until Monday to hear that, due to a totally unexpected and very localised heatwave, my hedgehogs were showing no sign of falling asleep and were, in fact, gambolling around like spring lambs. He would have to look elsewhere.

Just as it was getting dark on Sunday, there was a violent knocking on the front door. I opened it to find Nigel, a man I vaguely knew who lived in the next village, wrapped up against the biting wind and clutching a cardboard box.

'Sorry to disturb you on a Sunday, Mike,' he said, 'but we've just knocked down our old garden shed, ready to put up a new one. I took up the floor and there, underneath, was this big mound of grass and leaves.'

He opened the box and inside, curled into a tight ball, was a hedgehog. 'The new shed's got no room underneath for this fellow. I don't know what to do with it. You're the hedgehog man; can you help?'

The hedgehog was fast asleep; oblivious to the unfolding drama, it had already gone into hibernation ready for the onset of winter.

'No problem, I'll look after it.' I said, grabbing the box.

At five past nine the next morning I telephoned Ralph to tell him the good news.

'Excellent. Could you arrive about ten o'clock at studio six? Filming should only take a few hours and you'll be off again before the afternoon rush hour.'

That Thursday morning, the hedgehog was gently put into a huge box lined with masses of fresh straw and strapped, with a seatbelt, into the back seat of my car. Together we travelled down to London. To make absolutely certain that the hedgehog did not wake from its slumber the temperature inside the car had to be kept as low as possible: the car heater was switched to cool and the windows were wide open. The weather forecasters had been spot on with their predictions for that day. The late autumn sunshine had given way to a November cold snap. It was foul weather; wind howled around the inside of the car and rain lashed the windscreen. By the time we reached the BBC, I was frozen to the marrow. My hands were so cold they wouldn't co-operate anymore; I couldn't even hold onto the handle to close the windows. They were left open all day and I got back to a very wet driver's seat.

The receptionist at the BBC paged Ralph, who came to meet me at the front desk. I shook hands with blue fingers that were curled into talons by the 130 mile drive in near arctic conditions.

'My God man, you're freezing,' said the horrified Ralph, 'come and have a hot drink and breakfast in the canteen.' But before I succumbed to this achingly tempting invitation, we had to arrange accommodation for the hedgehog. He couldn't go into a warm studio until the very last moment. Ralph suggested we leave him in the gardeners' tool shed, which was unheated and fitted with a strong lock.

Satisfied that the hedgehog was safe, I tucked into bacon, sausage and eggs and gradually thawed out. This was the first paid job of my career; I

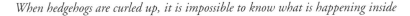

When hedgehogs are curled up, it is impossible to know what is happening inside

sat in the BBC canteen watching the famous wander past carrying their breakfasts. My fingers slowly regained their normal colour and I felt that life couldn't be better.

Ralph had asked me to go to Studio six after the meal, and I arrived at about half past ten.

'Sorry about this,' he said, 'but we're running a little late.' This statement should be tattooed on the brow of everyone who works in television. Running late is the usual state when filming; keeping exactly to schedule is a rare pleasure. But I didn't mind: this was a TV studio and I was there by invitation and being paid. I was happy to wait for days.

My hedgehog wasn't the first creature to arrive: a sleeping long-eared bat had been brought in earlier as another example of a hibernating animal. Studios are warm at the best of times and when the banks of giant lights are switched on the air temperature verges on the sub-tropical. Needless to say the bat had woken up. Even in a deep winter sleep, long-eareds are very sensitive to changes in the weather around, and in the wild will often come out of hibernation on warm winter days. It may have been at freezing point outside, but in the studio the temperature was like a warm afternoon in June. Under these conditions, the bat's metabolic rate had quickly increased causing it to wake up completely. The delighted creature was now zipping around the inside of the studio with effortless ease.

The bat's keeper was Murray, who ran a private bat hospital near London. He explained to me that the animal had been caught by a cat in Croydon; it had been badly mauled and needed stitches.

'It came to us in July and has only just recovered from the injuries. Normally they start to hibernate at the end of November; it's too late to release her now, so she can stay with us over winter and we'll release her in the spring.'

But the release had come earlier than planned. Long-eared bats are tiny creatures, smaller even than a mouse. The delicate animal was hard to see as she dived and darted around the lights and twisted through the spaghetti-like wiring. Bats are bright and agile: catching this hyperactive silhouette inside the cavernous studio was obviously going to be difficult.

The unfortunate Murray was, like everyone else, at a loss what to do next. From somewhere deep within the BBC's hidden nether regions a net was produced. I have since learned that the most extraordinary objects

14

are stashed in the prop rooms of the BBC and floor managers are rarely stumped when something unusual is needed. A telescopic microphone boom was taped to the short handle, to extend the net's reach. It was now about five metres long and about as manoeuvrable as a telegraph pole. For more than an hour various technicians, Murray and even the cameraman each tried their luck at capturing the escapee. The bat evaded all attempts with admirable panache; even when the gaping net was held directly in its flight path, with a sudden ninety degree jink or elegant sideways slip it would peel off at the last moment. The term 'blind as a bat' is a foul slur: they have surprisingly good eyesight and a sense of echolocation that we really cannot comprehend. Their ability to read information from a series of sounds bounced from surrounding objects is far more sophisticated and subtle than our own radar. Watching the performance I was deeply and, to be honest, selfishly grateful that hedgehogs can't fly and this was not my problem.

Catching the animal became a matter of honour. Almost everyone in the crew wanted the distinction of bagging the bat. Attempts became ever more daring. After a particularly frantic chase, the bat began to hover close to a speaker bolted to a steel beam high above our heads. Murray muttered,

'He's looking for somewhere to roost.'

Bats need something to cling to when resting; the speaker was covered with thick black material that would have been perfect for the animal's sharp claws to grasp. The bat was almost motionless in the air while the current challenger, an eager sound engineer, wielded the net silently beneath. With a wild overarm sweep that would not have been out of place on a cricket field he lunged at the bat with the net. He missed completely and with a horrible crunch hit a cluster of lights shattering three huge, and presumably expensive, silver bulbs. Shards of glass showered the concrete floor, while the bat joyously soared above us.

The frustrated director yelled, 'OK everybody, let's leave the damned bat alone and see if he settles down.'

High above, exploring every corner of the lofty studio heights, the bat was warm and thoroughly enjoying life. He had no intention of stopping for anyone.

After a hurried and whispered conference between the BBC crew and an increasingly depressed Murray, Ralph appeared and said, wearily, 'We're scrubbing the bat piece, we'll have to use some library footage instead. We've already lost too much time, so could you bring the hedgehog over and we'll set up?'

I collected the slumbering animal from the shed near the car park and gently carried him back to the studio. There I was introduced to a young man who obviously felt just as out of place as the bat-handler and I.

'This is Bob,' said Ralph, 'He's chief lab technician from the University. Bob's built a machine that can measure the heart rate and body temperature of your hedgehog, so we can show exactly what happens during hibernation. The trouble is we've run out of studio time. We're only booked in here for another hour; there's the hedgehog piece to record and then all the links to camera. We'll just have to fudge it a bit.'

The machine was an impressive device, about the size of a car battery. It was equipped with a mass of dials and knobs and had several wires running from the back of the box. On top was a printer equipped with two moving pens; it was already loaded with graph paper.

Bob explained that one wire was fitted with a sensitive probe that would be placed between the hedgehog's spines to record its body temperature. Another wire ended in a soft clip, which he would attach to a foot to count the pulse rate. Normally the machine would be connected for a few hours to show the exact pattern of the hedgehog's metabolism. But time was rapidly running short and Bob had to cut a few corners, or all of them to be more exact.

'I've been working with hibernating hedgehogs a lot in the past few years, we know their pulse rate slows from about 190 beats per minute down to 20 and their temperature drops to around 4 degrees centigrade.'

Bob was diligently working as he explained the plan; with enormous care he drew, completely freehand, two very faint lines across the graph paper. The top represented temperature and the bottom was pulse rate. He was no fool: neither line was completely straight. An animal's body doesn't operate as predictably as a machine; Bob deliberately drew in small peaks and troughs to show that both the pulse rate and temperature varied even when the hedgehog was in a deep sleep.

Sitting alone at the back of the studio the presenter was rehearsing his lines. I had watched this man many times before on wildlife programmes and now there was a chance to meet him. My hedgehog was whisked off into the centre of a studio and taken to a small set built to look like a zoology laboratory. Microscopes, test tubes and miscellaneous instruments surrounded the presenter. The set was brilliantly lit, and on the lab bench the hedgehog lay curled up on a bed of clean straw, right next to Bob's hibernation measuring device. Just before the camera started rolling, Bob stepped in and slid one wire between the hedgehog's spines and tucked the other behind an ear. Neither wire was connected to the animal and the machine was never actually turned on.

In just seven minutes the presenter competently explained the basic mechanisms of hibernation and, to illustrate his points, he used the graph paper which plotted every hiccup in the vital lifesigns of the comatose animal. The filming went without a hitch, but at the end the director asked if everyone could keep quiet 'for a few minutes' and stay in the studio while the last remaining links were recorded. These few minutes expanded into almost an hour. The hedgehog and box of technical wizardry had been moved out of the set and were left on a bench away from the filming action. Television work was not as exciting as I had imagined; the same sentences had to be shot over and over again when lines were fluffed. To pass the time I started examining Bob's gadget. The box was simple enough to use and I was interested to see it in action. I gently pushed the long metallic probe into the soft spines on the hedgehog's belly, and then fixed the padded clip onto its back leg.

The machine was switched on and gave out a very faint hum. The paper slowly rolled out leaving two thin traces where the twin pencils recorded precise information on the graph. The temperature measured 16 degrees, which was way too high for a hibernating hedgehog. But the really strange trace was on the pulse axis. The pencil stubbornly refused to move from zero. I had never used a gadget like this before and was probably doing something wrong. I took the clip off the hedgehog's ear and attached it to my own finger. Immediately the pencil registered a rate of 72 beats per minute; as I watched it suddenly rose up to 80, then 90 and finally over 100.

'Oh God, no, please no,' I said aloud, which earned a furious frown from the floor manager who was just then demanding silence ready for the next take. With a sickening plunge in my stomach I realised that the machine was working perfectly, but the hedgehog wasn't. With affected nonchalance I leaned down to scratch my ankle and as my head slowly passed the box, I took a deep sniff. The olfactory evidence was conclusive. The hedgehog wasn't hibernating – it was stone dead, and presumably had been for some time. Under the warm studio lights the fact was becomingly increasingly obvious. My career was ending before it had started; I had hired out a dead hedgehog to the BBC for what was, to me at least, an enormous amount of money.

Panic stricken, I pondered my next move when the director unexpectedly called out, 'OK, that's it for today. Thanks everybody, let's pack it all away.' I shall be eternally grateful to that man; he is one of the unsung heroes of my life. In my inexperience I hadn't realised that most television studios are just huge empty stages that change their appearance every day. At the end of filming the wildlife sets had to be completely cleared to make room for the props used by the next programme. The laboratory had to be dismantled quickly ready for a cookery show that was being recorded the following day. By now the bat had settled on one of the lighting gantries high up in the dark, hidden recesses of the roof space. He clung upside down on a thin wire, well out of reach. Murray wanted ten minutes alone in the studio to retrieve him, so the floor manager asked everyone to leave as soon as possible. I was only too delighted to be offered the chance to escape. The television crew disappeared in moments, leaving me to pack away the stiff, unmoving hedgehog. Clutching my box and walking briskly out through the giant studio doors, I caught a final fleeting glimpse of Murray scaling a wobbly ladder towards his sleeping quarry. I knew even then that he probably needed some help but it seemed wise to beat a hasty retreat before my dastardly deed was revealed. I never did learn if he managed to retrieve the errant bat.

Driving home it occurred to me that I should be racked with guilt over the fact that the BBC had been defrauded in such a gruesome and unique way. But, to be absolutely truthful, what really rankled was the memory of a journey in sub-zero temperatures, with the heater fan blowing cold and windows open, trying to prevent a dead hedgehog from waking up. My only solace was that, with the exception of the wet driver's seat, at least the return trip was a little more comfortable.

A few weeks later I switched on the television to watch the programme on hibernation. The piece opened with a misty and atmospheric film sequence showing a hedgehog rummaging around a woodland; the presenter explained how hedgehogs build up extra body fat during autumn, which will carry them through the months of winter. He went on to say that in October they look for somewhere quiet and dry to make a warm nest of leaves and grass. They then climb inside, curl up and sink into a deep, undisturbed sleep. Their body functions slow down until they reach a state that is as close to death as it's possible to achieve. The scene then changed to the horribly familiar studio laboratory set where the camera lingered on the hedgehog's motionless spines, to emphasise the lethargy of winter. The cameraman panned over to a high-tech shot of the metabolic recording machine with its twin tracks showing the hedgehog's slowed internal activity. I knew what was happening and still found it all very impressive. After demonstrating the workings of the disconnected gadget, the presenter finally turned to the camera and said with warmth and sincerity,

'It's about time we put the hedgehog back into its nest, although he won't wake up again until April. This chap will never even know he's been in a television studio.'

Well, I certainly couldn't argue with that statement.

He then gently laid the hedgehog corpse back into its box of straw and smiled at the audience as the end credits started to roll.

My income for that year was £39.00, and that was turnover, not profit. This sum was earned by hiring a dead hedgehog to the BBC. It was not an auspicious start. But it was a start and things could only improve.

2

Seat of Learning

There is one question that wildlife photographers hear more than any other: 'How on earth do you manage to get close enough to animals to take a picture?'

There is no straightforward answer to this very reasonable question. In a handful of rare and glorious places, like the Galapagos Islands, the wildlife is so ridiculously tame we can almost touch it, but sadly, in the rest of the world, very few animals are quite so co-operative. Most have learned, with very good reason, to fear man and keep as far away from us as possible. The vast majority of the world's wildlife photographs show the back ends of animals, disappearing over the horizon, taking up four percent of the picture. So wildlife photographers need to be downright devious if they are to bypass an animal's sensitive early warning systems.

Mammals are always the most difficult subjects; almost all have good hearing and eyesight but what makes them so frustratingly elusive is their incredible sense of smell. A mammal's nose will often detect the presence of danger long before its potential enemy is anywhere near. This is why most aspiring photographers first try their hand with birds, as they pose a less daunting problem. The vast majority have no sense of smell at all and we can take advantage of this design fault by sitting in a hide to take pictures.

A photographic hide is an invariably uncomfortable canvas tent barely large enough to house a human and his camera equipment. It is a masterpiece of minimalist design, consisting of four thin poles held up by guy-ropes pegged to the ground. The canvas is cunningly camouflaged with random splashes of soft greens and browns to help the unnatural sharp-edged box blend into the wild surroundings. A silent, unmoving human inside will be completely unnoticed by local birds even when they are, quite literally, sitting on top of him. Once inside the hide it is important to keep rock-still and not do anything that might catch the bird's attention and betray your presence. This inactivity is no problem for a short time but after about twelve hours it produces a little-recognised syndrome known in the trade as 'numb-bum'. The symptoms are unmistakable: a dull pain in the lower back, an absence of all sensation in the buttocks and an overwhelming desire to stand up and walk around. These must all be stoically ignored. However, the real key to successfully using a hide is simply not to drink anything before going in. Twelve hours inside a tiny canvas box can be excruciatingly unpleasant after three cups of tea with breakfast.

Wildlife photographers are always imagined to rely on telephoto lenses the size of bazookas, which allow us to stand on one side of a lake and take close-ups of an ant's left kneecap on the opposite bank. This kind of technology does exist, but it's depressingly expensive, heavy and awkward to use. In reality we tend to follow two very simple rules of thumb: get as close as possible and use a far more conventional camera. This approach often requires the help of a hide.

Hides are remarkably useful, but not totally foolproof. They have one major disadvantage: relatively speaking birds are tiny while hides are vast. If a large canvas box miraculously appears close to a bird's nest, the poor creature must feel as if a substantial hill has suddenly moved in next door. The hide may be small in our terms, but it is still more than thirty times taller than a robin and its instant, unannounced appearance is simply too intimidating for most birds to tolerate. Wild animals only accept the presence of a hide if it is discretely introduced; most are conservative and like to take their time to consider new phenomena.

On its debut appearance in a new site the hide is first built ten metres away from the nest, where it is just too remote to pose any threat. The odd structure doesn't move or make a noise, it doesn't fly or jump, the birds can see it but are not at all worried. Twenty-four hours later it is moved three metres closer, the following day another three metres and

on the fourth day it reaches the final position just two steps from the nest. The bird has now had plenty of time to look at the hide, think about it and finally ignore it. After four days the strange construction is completely accepted as just another innocuous part of the landscape. They treat it the same as they would a bush or fence. I've lost count of the number of times I have sat inside a hide, while a bird sits on top of the canvas roof or on a guy rope before hopping down to feed its chicks.

Photography from a hide only works because birds aren't terribly bright. When a potential enemy approaches a nest, the owners are quick to spot the impending threat. Although they seem to fly off in panic, they don't go far; once out of immediate danger they stop and sit in a distant bush. From this safe vantage point they carefully follow the intruder's every movement because a visible predator is far less dangerous than one that is hidden. The birds patiently watch and wait, and will not return to the nest until the enemy has definitely left. Photographers, being human, represent one of the most dangerous animals on earth; birds treat us with extreme mistrust. If a lone photographer walks to a hide, slips in and waits for the parents to come back and feed their chicks, he is doomed to failure from the start.

The nest owners, having seen him coming, will now be hiding in a bush carefully watching the proceedings. Birds don't understand the idea of entering a hide but they will see their terrible enemy suddenly disappear in front of their eyes. Because the menacing creature has not been seen to leave the area they know that he is still lurking, lethally close to their vulnerable nest. And, because the monster is now hiding, it is even more dangerous than it was before. The birds immediately become agitated and very frightened. They refuse to go anywhere near the nest until they are certain that the danger has passed. The terrifying creature has vanished but it hasn't been seen to leave, and there is a subtle but critically important difference between the two.

So the photographer sits inside the hide waiting for the bird to return, while the bird sits in a bush waiting for the photographer to leave – resulting in a stalemate. Luckily there is a ridiculously simple way out of this impasse, we just take advantage of the fact that very few birds can count – at all. Most have no mechanism whatsoever to tell the difference between one enemy and two. They can't count that high. Successful nest photography simply requires the brief help of an assistant. If two humans walk to a hide, one steps inside while the other noisily and very obviously wanders away, the silent watchers see danger arrive and then they see danger depart. The innumerate birds completely fail to notice the discrepancy in numbers; as far as they are concerned the momentary threat has provably vanished and it is now perfectly safe to return to the nest and carry on normal life. The conscientious creatures go about their chores blissfully unaware of the fact that, within arm's length, a human sits hidden inside a familiar, innocent part of their landscape. And, because the birds have no sense of smell, if the photographer keeps quiet and doesn't move he will never be discovered.

It's just as important to reverse the trick when it's time to leave the hide. If the bird is sitting peacefully on her eggs when a human appears, without warning, in front of the nest the results can be tragic. The bird suddenly realises that this area is hideously dangerous, because humans can magically emerge from the undergrowth without making their usual clumsy, heavy-footed approach. Birds have not thrived for million years by accident; they are quick to appreciate danger and know how to respond when threatened. A nest site where humans unexpectedly pop out is simply too hazardous to use. The parents' job is to raise chicks and, if they feel that their existing nest is compromised, they just abandon it and try a new spot where the chicks stand a better chance of surviving. When a nest is deserted the existing chicks or eggs soon die of cold or starvation, or are eaten by an opportunistic passing predator.

I learned the rules and pitfalls of hides with garden birds; photographing approachable, congenial species such as robins and blackbirds. But, like everyone in this field, I longed for a wilder background and more ambitious species. After three years working with small birds it became time to move on to new challenges and the greatest of these are birds of prey. By a stroke of good fortune I was invited to a small private estate in Scotland, a place which shall remain nameless to protect the extraordinary wildlife that lives there still. The owner was a keen conservationist who was trying to prove that shooting estates could provide plenty of birds for human hunters, while still offering shelter and a safe breeding ground for the native species of wildlife. He had been running the estate along these lines for several years and now wanted to write a magazine article that outlined his management techniques and philosophy. He needed some animal pictures to illustrate the article and I was given the job.

Although we had plenty of similar interests I never actually met the estate owner. Apparently few people ever did. He was a bit of a recluse and enjoyed the solitude of his moorland home. He was keen for me to track down his wildlife, but wasn't enthusiastic enough to bring himself to meet me in the flesh. He was only ever a remote voice on the telephone.

My contact on the project was Alec the head gamekeeper who ruled his empire with a rod of iron. He was only twenty-six and very young for the post; he had been employed because he represented the new breed of keeper who believed that all animals have a right to survive. Gamekeepers are paid to produce pheasants, partridges, grouse and sometimes deer; their job is to ensure that there are enough animals to guarantee a good hunt. In the past they were often paid according to the total number of birds shot by the end of the season. So shooting estates became production lines that were run on the same lines as factories, whatever the cost to the environment.

For two centuries traditional keepers viewed most wild animals as pests. If they weren't targets for the paying guests' guns then they were, by default, a threat to the gamekeeper's livelihood. Most would, at the drop of a hat, kill any bird with a hooked beak and almost every mammal larger than a vole. The resulting corpses were hung in tidy lines on grisly gibbets close to the road, proving to the landowners that the keeper was busily doing his job. This barbaric attitude lead to a huge slaughter of hawks, falcons, stoats, wildcats and almost every other native British predator, some were brought to the edge of extinction.

The irony is that this widespread massacre of predators probably resulted in an increased mortality of gamebirds. Carnivores don't just eat birds; a huge part of their diet is made up of small mammals. When most of the big predators vanished, their prey species went through a population explosion: there was nothing around to keep them in check. Rats have been in England for about a thousand years, brought in accidentally on trading boats from mainland Europe. For most of that time their population was controlled by efficient, native meat-eating animals but when gamekeepers wiped these out, the rats had a field day. In the nineteenth century their population simply mushroomed and this blossoming horde needed to eat. If there is one snack a rat really enjoys, it is a tasty, fresh egg or young chick. The rats probably killed far more pheasants and partridges than the predators that had been methodically wiped out to save those very same birds.

Modern keepers have a much more enlightened attitude; without a second thought some will still shoot animals that are proven to take their birds but the rest are untouched. Endangered species are usually completely left alone, even when they are seen picking off the occasional grouse. It is the hallmark of a good keeper when a healthy number of gamebirds lives alongside a thriving population of predators.

This philosophy paid handsome dividends for my mysterious patron, because his estate had became a prime site for hen harriers; a shy and increasingly rare bird that lives only on high, remote moorland. Over the first few weeks of spring, at the beginning of the project, I photographed curlews, bank voles and short-eared owls but it was the harrier that really captured my imagination. I had to wait sometime before turning to these birds, because hen harriers are protected by the law. Before even putting up a hide in its furthest position I first needed a licence that allowed me to approach the nest. All rare species in Britain have some degree of legal protection. It is not only birds that have this defence; the same law also covers rare mammals, insects and flowers. In a nutshell it is illegal to disturb any of these rare species; without a licence and under the terms of the law disturbance comes in many different forms. Shooting, trapping and handling are all forbidden, and so is photography. In the hands of a careless beginner, a camera can be a devastating tool. Photography can easily become a convenient excuse to harass an animal. An over-enthusiastic novice can leave a trail of deserted nests in his wake, making a hide just as lethal as a shotgun.

Rare and sensitive birds are sheltered from this risk by a nationwide licensing system that allows only experienced experts to approach their nests for study or photography. Licences are not granted lightly, applicants have to prove that they know exactly what they are doing, they must give referees and provide reams of other paperwork. The aim is not to stop the study of rare animals, but to try and ensure that the most threatened and sensitive species are free from disturbance by all but skilled naturalists. Anyone taking pictures of these animals without the right paperwork runs the risk of being heavily fined. When my licence eventually arrived, it granted me permission to photograph hen harriers but only on that particular estate and just during the month of June. It then expired.

Alec already knew of a suitable harrier nest, far out on the high moor, well away from the nearest road. It was an ideal site, well hidden from prying eyes. The hide was built thirty metres away from the nest. It was then covered with netting, into which were woven fronds of dead bracken and heather. The camouflaged canvas was soon covered in undergrowth making the hide virtually invisible from anywhere on the moor. It took ten days to move the hide slowly into its final position close to the nest. Early one morning Alec walked with me across the heather, waited while I stepped inside and then noisily strode off. It was then just a matter of waiting.

Through a tiny hole in the canvas I could see an untidy pile of twigs that looked as if they had just been picked up and carelessly abandoned by a random gust of wind. In the centre of the platform were three white eggs. The nest was built on the ground in a natural clearing; to every horizon there was a sea of knee-high heather bushes. These weren't the soft, gentle domestic plants on sale in garden centres, these were the tough, thick and weather-gnarled heathers of a high Scottish moorland and they did a perfect job of hiding the nest completely. The eggs were exposed to the sky but totally invisible to anyone at ground level. Apart from the occasional haunting, evocative call of a curlew, the moorland was silent. The viewing hole next to the camera was the size of my

From inside the hide the melancholic call of the curlew was the only sound I could identify with any conviction

thumbnail; there were nine thousand acres of hillside around but all I could see were two square metres of empty undergrowth.

A photographic hide is a sensory deprivation chamber; anyone sitting inside must keep absolutely still, not moving or touching anything. Sound is the only help in conjuring up a picture of events going on around, but after a while ears conspire with imagination to play unkind tricks. Wind-blown twigs constantly scratch on the canvas walls and sound just like animals creeping up behind. Creaking heather stems and voles scurrying through the undergrowth make mysterious noises: after a few hours inside a hide these scratches and scrapes can be interpreted in the most wild and unlikely ways.

The encircling sounds are very deceiving because when the real creature finally arrives, it is usually unannounced. The bird is careful not to draw attention to its vulnerable nest so it returns quietly and unobtrusively. With a soundless swoop the hen harrier landed on the edge of the twig pile. They may be birds of prey that kill for a living, but harriers are timid to the point of paranoia. As expected this was a female, and for a long time she stood with arched neck, carefully scanning the surrounding moor for signs of danger. For a few seconds she glared at the hide with unblinking golden eyes that glowed with eternal suspicion. One of the rarest birds in the country stood, just three strides away, completely unaware of my presence. At first glance hen harriers look like small eagles, but their beaks are not as powerful and they have a far less chunky build. The female is a soft mottled brown, which camouflages her beautifully as she crouches over eggs in the centre of an open moorland. Evolution has spared males these domestic duties, so they have no such need for secrecy; they are a flamboyant, amazing smoky grey colour that makes them look a completely different species.

The hide had worked its usual magic, this most wild of all birds had no idea she was being watched. Satisfied that nothing was about to attack, the harrier turned her attention to the all-important eggs. For the next month these tiny unmoving objects would be the focus of her universe. With precise care, she turned over each egg and pushed them together into a neat group in the centre of the platform. Urged on by an irresistible instinct to take care of her nest, the harrier, cocking her head from side to side, minutely examined every corner of the structure. She was particularly interested in the side nearest me and, after several close inspections, she obviously discovered a fault. The bird lowered her head to seize a small white feather and, with a dainty sideways flick, tossed it out of the nest. Content with her work she turned around and, in the process, swept her tail over the nearby heather and picked up the unwanted the feather. A few seconds later it slipped from her long tail and fell into the centre of the twig pile. The ever-alert harrier must have developed a personal grudge against this inoffensive feather because she noticed the security breach immediately. She stretched down and again tossed the abhorrent object out of the nest. This time it floated into the air and, caught by a whisper of wind, drifted downwards and landed on her neck. There it clung for a moment before sliding off once again to the floor. The house-proud bird was still slowly patrolling her domain and as the feather landed, put down her taloned foot where it instantly stuck. Eventually the bird was satisfied that the nest was habitable and set about checking her own appearance. The powerfully hooked beak meticulously combed the feathers on her chest until she caught sight of the delinquent feather. With a lighting-fast lunge the harrier picked up the feather, threw back her head and swallowed it whole. Using a pair of binoculars, the best that most people can hope to see of a hen harrier is a momentary swooping silhouette quartering the moor. This was a shy, aerial hunter of the wilderness, a bird that is desperately terrified of Man. Yet, hidden inside my tent, I watched her perform a surreal and unique ballet that was completely unseen by the rest of the world. Sometimes this job truly is a joy and privilege,an incredible opportunity to look into the secret world of wildlife. It is these moments that make the hard work worthwhile. DIY chores finished for the day, she then fluffed out her feathers and settled down on the eggs, her eyelids drooped and the elegant raptor drifted off to sleep.

Weather conditions are incredibly important to wildlife photographers and the forecast for that day was perfect. The local radio announced at six o'clock that morning that the weather would be dry and cloudy. This was ideal; the old adage about keeping the sun at your back was abandoned decades ago. Bright sunshine gives thick black shadows while high, light cloud produces wonderfully soft, diffused light. However this was the Hebrides, where conditions change at quicksilver pace and weather forecasting is more of a lucky dip than a skilled science. The first two hours went well, the hen harrier preened and bustled in gentle sunshine. She had her own timetable that consisted of sleeping for about twenty minutes and then housekeeping for ten. As the morning wore on glowering banks of dark clouds built up on the horizon. They steadily

Hen Harrier

crept across the entire sky and the view from my tiny peephole grew oppressively dark. At the stroke of ten o'clock the first raindrops fell. It started as light summer drizzle but quickly developed into a full Hebridean downpour.

Hides are tough and well built, they keep out showers and can even cope with hail but in my long and profoundly intimate experience with rain all around the world, that which falls in Scotland is unique. It is far more tenacious, determined and thoroughly vindictive than any other rain on Earth. A malignant wind appeared from nowhere and began to lash the rain against the thin canvas. Within a few minutes water started oozing through the roof in a dozen different places. Icy cascades trickled down my neck, others seeped into the bag of sandwiches and even the expensive 'waterproof' camera bags were eventually soaked. Through the curtain of driving rain I could just about see the hen harrier crouching low over her eggs. With head pulled down deep into her shoulders and eyes half closed, she couldn't have been any more wet if she had been thrown into a bath of water. The tiny feathers on her head were drenched; they stuck together in pointed clumps, giving her a hedgehog-like appearance. She looked as I felt – cold, wet and deeply fed-up.

The rain was relentless; I was soaked to the skin, and getting colder by the second. Anyone seeing this scene might ask, with good reason, why stay there? Why not just get out and find somewhere drier? The truth is that I would have dearly loved to return to my warm cottage with its crackling log fire but the hen harrier's welfare had to come first. They are acutely vigilant birds and the sodden female, sheltering her vulnerable eggs against the elements, had absolutely no idea that a human was so close. If I had simply clambered out of the hide and walked away, the sudden appearance of her worst enemy would have made the terrified bird fly off like a bullet from a gun. Harriers leave their nests if anyone comes within a hundred metres: a human materialising just two metres away would so traumatise the bird that she would have probably deserted the eggs. Even if she didn't completely abandon the site, it would have taken her so long to build up enough confidence to return that the rain would have chilled the eggs and killed the developing chicks inside. I just had to stay until the rain stopped.

There was no let up in the downpour, if anything it got harder and more bad-tempered as the afternoon progressed. Photography had come to a complete halt, the cameras were covered with a fine mist of condensation and the bird in front resembled a drowned rabbit. It's at times like this that wildlife photography loses its original charisma: I had been in this situation just too many times before. Cold, wet, bored and confined inside a claustrophobic box for another five hours, the idea of a radical career change became alluringly attractive. This wasn't the first time that I began scanning my mind for alternative occupations. But my daydream always got stuck at the interview stage. I could almost hear myself explaining,

'Well I can imitate tawny owls, climb trees, identify eleven species of bat, work for forty-eight hours without sleep, track mountain gorillas through bamboo forest, sit inside a tent all day without moving and, oh yes, I'm really good at finding rare species of lemurs.' Deep inside was the knowledge that there was only one job that needed such a strange assortment of arcane skills, and I was already doing it.

After one of the longest two hours of my life, I felt rather than heard a soft *snick, snick, snick* sound. The falling rain still thundered like chaotic drumbeats on the hide roof, so it was difficult to pinpoint exactly where this new noise came from. I thought at first that yet another leak had sprung and was dripping onto a sprig of heather. Unfortunately I was wrong. After a silent and comprehensive search I managed to track down the real source. The stitches on the nylon seat of my chair were breaking with metronomic regularity. Aluminium fishing stools are ideal for hides, they are comfortable and light to carry. But this one dated back to my college days and had long ago passed its sit-by date. It had been mended and patched so many times that the pattern on the original nylon seat was now unrecognisable. It should have been replaced years before and the frayed stitching had sadistically chosen that day to give up the struggle once and for all. Even though I knew exactly what was going on, I was powerless to stop it. *Snick, snick snick*, the last few stitches gave way and the seat came free from the aluminium crossbars that supported it. There was no great crash or dramatic lurch. Without the nylon seat to hold me up, slowly and inexorably I sank down into the small square frame. A few seconds later I was completely stuck, like a cork in a bottle.

My knees were forced up to my chest; this pushed my toes forward so that they touched the front of the hide. Each time I tried to scramble out, every movement made the canvas jerk around wildly. The infinitely wary harrier immediately noticed the unwelcome activity and her glittering eyes stared accusingly at the hide. If the canvas was flicked again, no matter how slightly, her nerve would break and she would fly off. I was physically and morally unable to move.

The front bar of the frame was a highly effective tourniquet that stopped the blood flow to my legs: in just ten minutes all sensation from the thighs downward had completely disappeared. Half an hour later I poked my calves with an iron hard heather twig and could feel absolutely nothing. It was as if the unmoving limb belonged to someone else. The rain pounded endlessly for another two hours and the seemingly harmless canvas hide became a torture chamber that felt, just at that moment, as if it would not have been out of place in a dark secret cellar controlled by the question masters of the Spanish Inquisition. My legs throbbed mercilessly, shooting pains catapulted into my thighs and, no matter how hard I tried, my toes would not produce even a minor twitch. By leaning slightly to one side, I could rest a tiny part of one buttock on the ground, relieving some of the weight from the unforgiving, vicious seat frame. The downpour had turned the soil into a sea of mud; my only contact with the earth was through an ice-cold pool of murky water. This brought an entirely new meaning to the phrase 'numb bum'.

Fortunately even Hebridean storms finally blow themselves out and, as quickly as it had appeared, the rain thankfully stopped. By then the hen harrier was literally soaked to the skin. Bird feathers are coated with an oil that keeps them dry in showers but even they cannot cope with deluge on that scale. Instead of keeping off the water, the bird's feathers eventually started to absorb it. When the dark clouds finally evaporated and gave way to thin sunshine, the patient harrier stood up and cascades of water dropped from her beak and tail. With flattened feathers plastered down to her skin, the bedraggled bird looked about half the size she was ten hours earlier. The harrier then gave a mighty shake, vibrating her body in sections starting with her head and shoulders, then working down to the long wet tail. Water spun off her plumage and a few droplets landed on the front of my lens. Once again, she started to look like a true predator. The harrier took a long look around the horizon and then lay down on the nest with her wings spread out, arched towards the strengthening sun. Faint wisps of steam began to drift up from her drying feathers: she was obviously enjoying herself. After about an hour of sunbathing the bird was dry once again; then she stood up, walked off the nest and silently took to the air. The harrier was ravenously hungry after her cold, wet vigil. She had gone off in search of the countless voles and mice that made their home in the surrounding heather.

With her out of the way at least I could wrestle a bit more freely with the evil chair but, as my legs now totally refused to move, there was little I could do until help arrived. For all I knew the harrier could well be searching the moorland right behind the hide; I still couldn't take the chance of moving too much. Alec had helped me into the hide early that morning and had strict instructions to come and get me out at six in the evening. I was due to be inside for ten hours that day and, after the tender ministrations of the monstrous chair, it felt more like ten days. The last few minutes before release crept past slower than time has any right to move. I strained to hear the sound of distant boots pushing through the tangled undergrowth. But, apart from the occasional call of a curlew, there was not a single noise to be heard.

'Are you all right in there?' came a soft-voiced inquiry from the other side of the canvas. I had forgotten that Alec was professionally silent. His job was to move around the estate without disturbing, or being noticed, by the wildlife. He had long ago learned to cross a moorland and not make a sound.

'Get me out of this bloody thing,' I groaned.

Alec unzipped the door and peered inside.

'Does that help your photography?' he said, without a trace of irony.

I rolled over onto my side and fell out of the opened door. Alec pulled the chair and the aluminium relinquished its maniacal grip. The blood rushed back into my legs with a pounding agony. Losing circulation had been bad enough but having it return was infinitely worse. A forest of red-hot needles seemed to invade my flesh. My knees gave way and dropped me into the soft heather. It was about ten minutes before I could stand up and walk. Even then it was a travesty: my legs refused to straighten up and each one seemed to weigh more than a small car. We needed to leave the nest area quickly, photography had finished but the harrier still had work to do incubating her eggs. Alec carried my bags as I hobbled over the moor doing a better than average imitation of Quasimodo after a hard day in the bell-tower. In the bath that evening I could clearly see the thick red wheals across the back of my thighs where the chair frame had trapped them for nearly four hours. It took about forty-eight hours for my legs to return to normal.

That was almost the last nest I ever worked on. Ostensibly I gave up this particular field of photography because the nesting habits of every species had been well documented: there was no real need to spend more time recording behaviour that had been thoroughly explored. But today I have to accept the fact that the reprehensible and degenerate chair played a major part in this decision.

3

On The Trail of the
Lonesome Pine Marten

Some animals have more popular appeal than others. It may be unfair but it is true. Most people prefer creatures that are cuddly or cute over those that are slimy or are the owners of an uncomfortably large number of legs. Which is why, in a zoo, the scorpion house is deserted while eager and cooing crowds flock to see the pandas. It can be frustrating to see the random winners and losers in the wildlife popularity stakes and know that it is all based upon a skin-deep appearance.

But with the best intentions even hardened professionals have their own favourites and, despite trying to stay impartial, I have to own up to being equally guilty of the crime. In Britain, for me at least, the pine marten is one animal that is utterly irresistible. Related to badgers, stoats, otters and their kin, pine martens are rare and elusive creatures. They are also one of the most magnetically attractive of all wild mammals. The combination of scarcity and beauty make pine martens popular subjects with publishers. For too many years this species was at the top of my wish list, but I failed miserably even to see one, let alone take any photographs. Then, by complete accident, I heard about a forester on the west coast of Scotland who fed wild martens in his garden. I wangled an invitation and arranged a trip to a remote hamlet on the Ardnamurchan peninsula. This huge chunk of land is the most westerly point of mainland Scotland; it begins at the base of Ben Nevis and points out into the open Atlantic Ocean. Few people live in this wild landscape: the nearest town of any size is Fort William, and that is well over an hour's drive from some of the coastal villages.

Wilderness, in the form of forest and heather moorland, dominates the countryside. On Ardnamurchan red deer outnumber humans by maybe two to one, and golden eagles constantly sweep the skies. Twice a day, following the ebb tide, otters skitter along the beaches searching through rafts of seaweed abandoned by the high water. Looking for crabs lurking in the damp weed, they nose around the sand investigating interesting smells and prying with inquisitive finger-like forefeet. Crabs are leapt on with gusto and the sound of cracking shells can be heard echoing around the bays that make up the meandering coastline.

Inland from the beaches, on the lower slopes of bare-topped hills, nestle patches of ancient forest where, amongst the red squirrels and occasional wild cats, the pine martens live. About the size of a cat, pine martens are a wonderfully rich chestnut colour and have a scrupulously clean cream-coloured patch on their throat and chest. Three hundred years ago they could have been found over most of Europe, but a combination of the relentless destruction of their habitat and a savage slaughter at the hands of nineteenth-century gamekeepers has driven the last few animals to remote strongholds where humans are rare.

In quiet Scottish forests pine martens live unnoticed and undisturbed by people. They have learned to stay away from Man; even in good

Otter

marten areas they can be frustratingly elusive. Under a blanket of darkness they climb and leap silently through high branches, hunting birds and small nocturnal animals such as voles and mice.

Judith, my wife, and I arranged to stay for a week in late November. After a never-ending drive we finally arrived at an old cottage that was hidden among ancient wind-twisted trees on the side of a sea loch. The house was completely invisible from the road; it could only be reached by a winding bumpy lane through the gloriously unkempt garden. The cottage was more than two hundred years old and had started life as a crude fisherman's shelter, but since then it had been extended and modernised. It may have been well off the beaten track but, equipped with colour television and central heating, this was obviously going to be one of our more luxurious destinations. The forester was away for the weekend, so we settled in quickly and started exploring. Our first night in Ardnamurchan was spent wandering the oak forest behind the house looking for pine martens. Two animals were known to live there all year round and probably more would occasionally pass though on hunting excursions. But knowing where pine martens live is no guarantee at all that it will be possible to find them in the flesh.

The search didn't start until after nine o'clock in the evening. It takes about half an hour for human eyes to become sensitised to the darkness after leaving a brightly-lit room. Our eyes are designed to work in daylight and are slow to get used to the dark. I long ago learned that it's better to take a little time to let my eyes become accustomed to the night than to cut corners and use a torch. Nocturnal animals have infinitely better sight than we do: they can probably see the bright artificial light of a torch up to a mile away and will go to extraordinary lengths to avoid it. It is a beacon in the night that warns every animal to stay away. Relying on a torch also means that our eyes never have the chance to become tuned in to the darkness so we only see what is caught in the beam of light and miss everything else. Carrying a torch I always feel like an intrusive outsider trying to look into the hidden nocturnal world, unable to spot the really interesting bits of the forest. We sat on a dry stone wall for nearly an hour while our night sight sharpened.

By ten o'clock we could just about see the stark silhouette of leafless winter trees against the dark sky. All we had to do then was find a wild pine marten.

'There's one over there. Look,' I whispered.

'No it's not,' said Judith, 'it's just an old branch.'

Shadows leaped and skulked around us, all conspiring to look exactly like pine martens. But they always turned out to be clumps of bracken, tree stumps and, once, a dead lamb. Pine martens are wary creatures with quicksilver ears and noses; after less than an hour we realised that we would not outwit martens on their own territory. This approach had never seemed very likely to work; luckily we had an alternative plan.

In the cold, never-ending damp of a Scottish winter, wild animals need to eat constantly to stay alive. It is ironic that the animals' energy requirements are at their highest at precisely the time when the food supply is at its lowest. Much of the martens' prey disappears in the autumn and doesn't return until the spring. Some birds fly south to avoid the worst of the weather; small mammals have enough trouble staying alive, so they stop breeding in winter. The inexperienced young voles and mice that make up so much of the martens' diet are nowhere to be found. Animals die in huge numbers during winter. The young, old and weak just can't cope with the bad weather so the population of all species is at rock bottom. But even in these conditions the remaining predators must still hunt every day to survive.

During the warm summer months, when food is plentiful and life is easy, martens are choosy feeders and only eat freshly killed prey. But they can't afford to be quite so fussy in winter and will try almost anything that offers a vaguely edible meal. If they find a good and reliable food supply, pine martens will come back to it again and again. Wildlife photographers often use this behaviour to their advantage and everyone benefits: the animals have a free meal and we get the pictures.

Campbell, the forestry warden who owned the cottage, shared my delight in pine martens. He had been watching them for more than twenty years, as part of his job and as a hobby. When he first took the job in Ardnamurchan, he urgently needed to find somewhere to live. There aren't too many houses around there and he had a frustrating quest that lasted several months before eventually finding a cottage that was, by pure chance, fully equipped with resident pine martens. Like any sensible man, he took the place immediately. I had only ever spoken to him on the telephone and the very first thing he told me was 'I didn't like the house very much. I still don't. The ceilings are low and it's too far from anywhere. But who, in their right mind, could turn their backs on the martens?'

Campbell moved in during a typically wet February and that night, in the confused debris of a household still packed away in boxes, he had a hurried supper of cold pie and baked beans. The unappetising meal was never finished and just before midnight was scraped onto the ancient bird table at the far side of the lawn. Next morning, as he surveyed his estate, the delighted Campbell spotted and recognised distinctive oval footprints in the mud around the bottom of the table. During the night opportunistic martens had come into the garden drawn by the seductive smell of stale steak and kidney pie. It was mid-winter and they would have been very, very hungry. The martens ate every scrap. Later that day Campbell reasoned if a bird table works, why not make a pine marten-table? Just before sunset, he put out a pile of assorted scraps on his huge stone step outside the back door. Over more than two centuries, generations of fishermen and their families had worn a smooth hollow into the giant slab as they walked in and out of the tiny back door. Unintentionally they had created a perfect natural bowl in which to leave food.

At first the martens were very wary, unwilling to venture this far onto enemy territory. The bird table, where they had eaten the night before, was a long way from the house but the doorstep was perilously near and permeated with the scent of humans. Pine martens have a keen sense of smell and could clearly detect the frightening stench of Man mingled with the tantalising aroma of food. The competing senses of fear and hunger would have made the animals extremely nervous. But, in the end, the overwhelmingly strong smell of food was too strong to ignore. Sitting inside the house at one o'clock in the morning, with all lights switched off, Campbell watched as a low, fast shadow darted out of the gloom, quickly grabbed the food then vanished back into the night. The culprit was almost invisible in the darkness, and, when it ran off, left more than half the meal on the doorstep. The following evening the animal stayed a few seconds longer and cleaned up each last crumb with its long tongue.

Over the next few months the pine marten visited every day shortly after dusk. It became a predictable ritual; Campbell's doorstep was its first point of call in the nightly quest to find food. That particular winter was unusually harsh and the food no doubt helped keep the animal alive. When spring finally arrived, and the weather grew warm, the marten became a less frequent visitor. In this gentle season there is no difficulty finding food; the marten would have felt it was time to turn his attention to the business of breeding. For more than five months the pine marten stayed away and Campbell knew it would be hidden deep in the woodlands, close to a hollow tree trunk containing a nest of three growing young. When the first frosts of the winter bit in late October, life in the forest grew more difficult. One ice-cold night, pine marten tracks once again appeared around the bird table. It was time to put out food on the doorstep.

Pine martens are meat-eaters but they are not obsessive: they will happily take a variety of other titbits whenever the chance arises. Fish, birds' eggs, worms, beetles, caterpillars are all part of their normal diet. In the autumn they enthusiastically eat ripe wild blackberries and have even been known to raid gardens for raspberries. When trying to work out the menu for the doorstep feast, Campbell tested the obvious foods that he thought should tempt a hungry marten. At first he left out bacon fat and chicken scraps: they were eaten but not always finished. Sometimes they were totally rejected and the meal would still be there in the morning. He wanted to find a food that would really appeal to the animals, a meal that would be guaranteed to bring them into his garden every night.

Campbell logically worked out that he should offer them something special; treats that they really enjoyed but couldn't normally find. Being carnivores they ate meat almost every day so chicken and bacon scraps were hardly likely to set their hearts racing. Like most mammals, including we humans, pine martens have a passion for sweet foods. In the wild, ripe autumn berries are the sweetest morsel animals ever get to eat. Sooner or later everyone in Campbell's position eventually discovers that sugar, in all its forms, is the ultimate bait. Even the most suspicious creature can be lured by the scent of sticky puddings. He tried offering all sorts of unlikely snacks to the martens: dog biscuits mixed with honey, cold treacle tart and peanut butter sandwiches smeared with chocolate spread were all left on the doorstep. Each exotic delicacy was eaten but not with the wild abandon he expected.

After almost a year of dedicated trial and error he finally found the perfect irresistible recipe. One dark damp December evening Campbell discovered the formula for the supreme pine marten supper – raspberry jam and sultanas. For the average wild pine marten on the west coast of Scotland these are rather elusive commodities and the sugar-hungry animals would do almost anything for the chance to feed on this strange combination, and that includes visiting gardens.

The bait was a potent cocktail; soon pine martens were being attracted from ever further into the woodland. Campbell's garden became a marten Mecca. Five were seen one evening scuttling in the shadows waiting for an opportunity to grab their own mouthful of juicy sultanas, glued together with sticky raspberry jam. By the time Judith and I arrived, the hard work had all been done; the doorstep bait was a magnet to the local martens. By now Campbell could identify most of the individual animals that came to eat. They each had tell-tale scars or markings that separated them from the others. Pine martens are aggressively territorial in the breeding season but in winter they were less willing to fight. Deliberately to avoid confrontation the martens came at different times and were uncannily accurate in keeping to their own schedule every evening. All we had to do was wait.

There was just one subtle difficulty. Campbell had always fed the animals on his doorstep, so that he could sit inside the warm house and watch them through the huge floor-length window. It would have been very simple to photograph them on their usual dining table. But, zoologically speaking, portraits of wild pine martens sitting on a doorstep lack a certain realism and authenticity. Squirrels and hedgehogs look perfectly at home amongst tended flowerbeds and neat lawns, but pine martens are mystical and elusive creatures of the night woods and should look the part. The pine martens couldn't be moved to the forest so we had to bring the forest into the garden.

The first full day in Ardnamurchan was spent searching for fallen trees and branches; I was looking particularly for long-dead logs that were rotting and covered with lichens and moss. The prettiest were collected and carefully carried back to Campbell's cottage. There, outside the back door, they were cunningly put together to recreate a quiet corner of woodland. Log arranging is just one of the highly specialised and otherwise useless skills necessary in wildlife photography. The background must appear natural, as if it had slowly accumulated over decades and not just tipped out of the back of a wheelbarrow ten minutes earlier. Once the logpile looked convincingly realistic, finishing touches were added in the form of branches from Scots pine trees draped picturesquely around the mound. Fronds of autumnal golden bracken and bramble were carefully wedged between the logs. The whole stage was then liberally sprinkled with handfuls of pine needles, cones and dead leaves. By sunset, in Campbell's garden, we had built an exact replica of the interior of a Caledonian forest – the scene was set.

The quick-witted martens had long ago learned where to find supper, but that night the garden was different; the food had moved and they needed to be led to their new dining table. We put some of the fattest sultanas on the doorstep and then laid a trail of the rest leading to the log pile. In the kitchen Judith prepared a meal of raspberry jam and sultanas then, using a knife, she stuffed the heady mixture into cracks between the logs and covered it with leaves. Just before dusk fell, I settled down in the opened kitchen door and waited. Nocturnal animals can see extremely well in the dark, but they do have an Achilles' Heel: they cannot detect red light. Evolution has produced eyes that work efficiently in low light but are not terribly sensitive to colours, particularly at the red end of the spectrum. An ordinary white-light torch would be an unfamiliar sight that would keep the pine martens away from the house, but light from a small table lamp fitted with a red bulb was completely invisible to them.

Wearing a woolly hat and gloves, with a thick duvet over my knees, I sat on the cold stone doorstep and watched the garden. Bathed in an eerie glow, the scene was surreal. Deep shadows still looked black but everything else appeared to be various shades of red. The concrete path leading from the house to the woodshed was deep scarlet and the normally pale stone doorstep seemed positively bloodstained. The martens would certainly be late tonight: my strange activities in the garden would make them a bit more apprehensive than usual and I knew it could be some time before they appeared. In the dark silence of a night garden, our normal senses are robbed of information, eyes can't be trusted and imagination takes over. Wildlife watchers are always desperate to see something and, all too often, optimism plays dirty tricks. 'Was that

shadow over on the left really there five minutes ago? Did it just twitch?'
All around there seemed to be the slowly stalking shapes of hungry pine
martens; shapes that in reality never actually moved.

As I grew increasingly cold and stiff, the pine martens adamantly
refused to put in an appearance. Two hours later, there was a movement
behind the logs. I switched on the camera and held my breath. Suddenly
a wood mouse darted out, seized a sultana, and vanished under a bush.
Thirty seconds later it was back to grab another. Over the next twenty
minutes this mouse, and probably several of his friends, collected the
entire sultana trail. My carefully laid plans had been thwarted by a horde
of rampaging rodents. It was too risky to walk over and lay more bait:
the martens may already have been in the garden. Any movement would
probably have frightened them off.

For the next hour nothing happened and it's at times like this that,
completely unprompted, the question pops into my mind, 'What am
I doing watching a pile of rotting logs? It's the middle of a cold and
damp night, every other sensible person on the face of the earth is
roasting chestnuts on an open fire with their hands curled around a mug
of hot chocolate.' I strongly believe that all healthy, practising wildlife
photographers frequently experience doubt about the sanity of their
chosen profession.

Suddenly a small shadow moved at the far end of garden; with an
inward sigh I realised that it was probably just another shrub taking a
stroll. Slowly the low silhouette grew larger and a pair of magnetic ruby
eyes emerged, caught in the dull red glow of the lamp. A small triangular
head peered tentatively around the edge of the log pile. It was a cat......a
cat! I had waited three hours in the cold for a lousy cat. It was a strange
looking animal with a distinctive grey and orange coat. It lived in a
cottage on the edge of the wood. By sheer co-incidence I had seen it
earlier that day and knew that it was far from home and on unfamiliar
territory. With each carefully placed step the cat stopped and peered
around; it was obviously nervous and needed just a gentle nudge to
persuade it to leave. A shout would have driven it away, along with any
pine marten that happened to be nearby. A few years before I'd written
a book on owls and only then discovered a previously hidden talent to
mimic their calls. An angry *kew-wick, kew-wick* pierced the silent garden.

One of the piratical woodmice that almost thwarted my plans

The cat froze in horror and, with ears twitching wildly, stood transfixed for a few seconds, then the panic-stricken creature turned tail and fled into the gloom. It had no intention of tangling with a fully-grown tawny owl that seemed to be sitting on the ground just a few steps away. That wasn't the first or last time my owl impression had avoided the unwanted attentions of small animals. The cat had been frightened away but the martens would be completely unconcerned by the presence of a bird that they could easily kill if necessary.

Thirty seconds later the pine marten materialised with almost supernatural stealth: there wasn't a sound, just a faint flickering shadow before the animal stepped onto the logs. I had completely misjudged its abilities: the marten had no need to follow the sultana trail. Equipped with a sense of smell so sensitive we can't really understand how it works, the animal knew exactly where its food was hidden. I had pored over every available book on this species before coming to Scotland, but these just hadn't prepared me for the stunningly beautiful creature that stood almost close enough to touch. About the size of a fox, pine martens have pointed dog-shaped faces with sharp erect ears. They are elegant and move with a silent cat-like grace. The marten delicately sniffed the logs, nuzzled a few leaves out of the way with its nose and eagerly sucked up the sticky meal. Its glossy coat looked almost crimson in the red lamplight.

When I pressed the button to fire the camera, the garden was brightened for a thousandth of a second by the electronic flash. The marten idly looked around for a moment and went back to the serious matter of eating. This food was a luxury to be savoured and the marten was in no hurry. It settled down on the logs, with a long bushy tailed curled around its feet: a ceremony that had been followed almost every night for the past three months. With painstaking thoroughness, the marten probed each possible hiding place; with a sensitive and impressively long tongue he unearthed every scrap of the luscious treat. Once the food was finished he spent a few seconds lazily licking his lips and front paws. Then, without a sound, the marten vanished into the blackness, back into his own world. I took half a roll of film that evening, and went to bed a happy man. There is nothing quite like a good session with a wild pine marten for keeping out the cold of a November night.

I watched the pine marten every night for more than a week. For all I know it may possibly have been several different animals. I didn't have Campbell's skill in identifying individuals in the dark. During those cold, draughty sessions on the doorstep, I fell hopelessly in love with pine martens. They are delicate, agile, beautiful and depressingly rare. It was a real privilege to see them at such close quarters.

When next you see a photograph of a pine marten published in a book, study it closely. The animal will be probably be standing against the backdrop of a pristine Scottish forest. The bracken will be crisp and damp; the marten will no doubt be sitting on an ancient log dripping with moss, lichens and fungi. It's tempting to believe that the intrepid wildlife photographer has crawled on hands and knees through the wild woodland. Night after night, through the mud, cold and gloom, he endlessly searches for the country's most elusive animal. After weeks of unrequited patience his pains are amply rewarded when the marten appears for a fraction of a second, just long enough to allow one photograph to be taken, before disappearing wraith-like into the darkness. That is exactly the evocative image we aim for. I can almost guarantee that the pine marten in the picture is completely wild – but the 'forest' is designer built. There will not be a tuft of moss or sprig of bracken out of place; each log will have been carefully chosen and artistically arranged with the skill of an interior decorator. And what you can't see, stuffed in every available nook and cranny, hidden from view, is the contents of a bag of sultanas and two jars of the finest raspberry jam.

4

Life in the Fast Lane

A few years ago, via a series of recommendations along a very convoluted chain of friends and colleagues, I had a telephone call from a producer working in American television. He was making a series of programmes looking at the ways humans constantly manipulate the natural world and how animals are obliged to react to these continual changes. This is one of the core issues of modern conservation. Some species are so specialised that they cannot tolerate even the smallest alterations in their habitat while others are born survivors that can make their home in the most unlikely spots.

This was a major new TV series and camera crews all over the world were delving into a whole range of contemporary stories. One cameraman was filming house mice in the Antarctic; these were once stowaways accidentally carried south in boxes of provisions to feed the small army of scientists stationed on this inhospitable continent. Once there, the mice were trapped in research station buildings: they could not venture outside into temperatures that would kill them in a matter of minutes. But the mice still managed to thrive and breed, kept alive by the same completely artificial environment designed to support the scientists. Other crews were filming grizzly bears living on giant rubbish tips, racoons breeding in chimneys in Maryland and snowy owls hunting on the runways of Toronto airport.

My part of the project was to film those few enterprising animals that had learned to live on motorway verges – a place where, it is tempting to think, no-one would ever seriously look for wildlife. The only animals usually associated with motorways are those spread across the carriageway, having tried – and abysmally failed – to cross. Verges seem to be just long, sterile strips of dull undergrowth that shadow a noisy, smelly, never-ending stream of traffic. But in reality verges are one of the unlikely hits of the conservation world, a new environment that took us all by surprise. Originally they were designed as a pragmatic buffer zone between the surrounding landscape and the speeding traffic. No-one gave much thought to the colonising effect of nature. In the decades since the first British motorway was built in the 1950s hundreds of species of wild flowers have appeared, grown from seeds carried by the wind or caught on birds' feet. Today the range of plant life on a well-established verge can be amazing, supplying food for birds, mammals and insects in areas where their traditional landscape might be slowly vanishing. The endless grassy strips have unintentionally become long thin nature reserves that are alive with countless animal species. But, isolated inside a car hurtling past at seventy miles an hour, few people ever see them.

Wildlife is free to come and go while humans are legally forbidden to set foot on the grass. Motorway verges are now a secluded, rich habitat that, in total, covers more than twice the area of all Britain's National Parks put together. They are almost completely free of disturbance, if the animals can only learn to tolerate the presence of the relentless roar of vehicles. The voles, shrews and mice living next to the tarmac are certainly aware of their surroundings. They can see, hear and smell the traffic. Small mammals are also very tactile; they have an acute sense of touch that feels the vibrations created by thundering lorries passing by. But none of these man-made sensations seems to deter them. Some of the small resident mammals are now the two-hundredth generation of their kind to live on a verge. It must be as familiar to them as a woodland is to a badger.

In earlier times the countryside worked at a sedate, more civilised pace. There were no real machines; milking and harvesting were slow manual jobs. Nineteenth century farms were home to a huge number of animals. Cereal fields – full of wheat, corn and barley – were an ideal habitat for mice and voles. Life was straightforward: they fed on the cultivated plants and easily avoided close contact with man, simply because they had time to see us coming and run. Today's farms are much more mechanised and efficient. While it once took an army of labourers four days to bring in the harvest from just one small field, today a single man, driving an air-conditioned giant harvester, can do the same job in a few hours. This has accelerated the danger and made life much more hazardous for small

Rabbits are not a native species: they were introduced to Britain in the eleventh century. Highly adaptable, they can can make their home anywhere, even in motorway verges

animals, because they have far less time to escape the slicing blades and crushing wheels. Many have moved away from this danger zone and taken up residence in less traumatic habitats – such as roadside verges.

The motorway system of Britain is not just a profitable place to find food and shelter; it has grown to become an interconnected web of narrow corridors that allows wildlife to move around unnoticed. This silent animal subculture uses motorways in the same ways as we do; they can wander freely, explore new places and enter cities, without ever being seen. Beneath the shelter of tangled grass, blown and twisted by traffic-driven winds, there is an entire world of small animals hidden from view.

For the motorway project, the first task was to apply for yet another essential licence: one that allowed me onto the verges. It is illegal to stop on a motorway unless there is an accident or breakdown. After filling in a small mountain of paperwork and a wait of several weeks my licence eventually arrived from the Department of Transport: at last I was legal and ready to start work.

Just to get a feel of the habitat, without even taking a camera, I drove to the nearest stretch of motorway, parked the car and sat on the verge with a pair of binoculars. My first reaction was horror – there was rubbish everywhere. Cigarette packets, drink tins, newspapers and even old shoes stretched to infinity in both directions. They could not be seen by passing traffic, because most had obviously been lying there slowly decaying for years and had become almost part of the undergrowth. No-one visits motorway verges and that includes street cleaners.

While the licence application was being processed, I spent many hours reading the inevitable reports drawn up by various government departments responsible for the building and upkeep of motorways. Hidden amongst the mountain of diagrams, pie charts and tables was a list of the trees that had been planted on verges when the roads were first built. Trees are vital to the workings of a motorway: their large and complex root systems help bind together the banked earth that makes up most verges. They also act as efficient sound-breaks that muffle the noise of traffic, which is important when the motorway goes through built-up areas. Trees also soften the harsh, unforgiving appearance of the endless carriageways that scar the landscape, making them look a little more acceptable.

The report listed blackthorn, hawthorn, hazel and a surprisingly wide cross-section of the smaller British trees. But walking along the verge for the first time, the one species that stood out more than any other was apple. There was no mention of these ever being planted on roadside verges yet here they were, growing in their dozens. Where on earth had they come from? After a few seconds musing I realised that although this was an interesting mystery it wasn't helping my filming. So I tucked myself under a hawthorn bush and sat quietly to watch the road and verge, to get an idea of typical daily life. I was in camouflaged clothes, so that the animals wouldn't be alarmed by the unique presence of a human in their normally secret world. It also, unintentionally, hid me from the migrating drivers.

At first the noise of roaring traffic was deafening but as I got absorbed in the comings and goings of solitary magpies and busy starling flocks searching for food amongst the untidy vegetation, the cars were eventually forgotten. Until the moment an apple core rifled out from an open window, streaking past at 70 mph. The half-gnawed core bounced on the hard shoulder and landed on the grass close to my feet. It also instantly resolved the riddle of the unexplained saplings. The apple trees on the verge hadn't been intentionally planted – they were the product of our appalling habit of throwing rubbish around. I would love to come back in fifty years time, just to see if the motorways of Britain will become fringed with long, thin orchards stuffed full of Cox's Orange Pippins, Golden Delicious and Braeburns. It was an irresistible mental image.

While deliciously immersed in this glorious picture of the motorways' fruitful future, I noticed a movement in the grass. The brown, furry head of a vole emerged cautiously from beneath the remains of a rusty, long-dead exhaust pipe hidden in the undergrowth just a few steps away from me. The tiny, oil-black, beady eyes scanned the horizon; the twitching, whiskery nose scented the air carefully before the vole suddenly catapulted out into the open, scurried through the grass and disappeared into a bank of nettles. Luckily the wind was blowing into my face, carrying my tell-tale human smell away from the wary creature.

A second later the tiny vole stormed out and grabbed the core. The flesh had already turned an unappealing dark brown colour but it was this very change that attracted the animal's attention. Freshly cut apples give out little smell, but as they go brown the scent ripens and becomes stronger. All rodents love apples in any form and the sweet, cloying odour would have been a powerful magnetic advert. These particular pips would never have the chance of germinating and growing to join the motorway orchard; the hungry vole would eat every scrap of the core.

Being so low down on the food chain, the vole was instinctively aware that out in the open he may well be pounced on by any one of a long list of predators; it wasn't safe to eat away from the protective umbrella of thick undergrowth. The vole grabbed the core with his sharp little teeth and, using short jerking pulls, started to drag the meal backwards towards the nettles. Every so often he stopped for a moment and looked around for signs of danger; voles have lightning fast reactions and he would have vanished at my slightest movement. Fascinated by the struggle, I stopped breathing, in case my gently moving chest signalled that something ominously big was watching. The apple core looked larger than the vole so the animal really had to work for this feast. It would be the same as me trying to pull a gas cooker across a football field without any help. This brown rodent was no bigger than my thumb and I suddenly realised that, for its relative size, the tenacious creature was phenomenally powerful. Eventually the vole reached the nettle bed and reversed into its secure darkness, hauling its dinner behind. The whole drama had been completely hidden from the stream of traffic less than two steps away.

Drivers may never see these tiny animals but not all species are as unobservant as humans. Where there is a large population of small furry creatures concentrated in any one spot, somewhere nearby is an army of sharp-eyed hunters that are doing their very best to eat them. Stoats and weasels long ago learned to patrol the verges for food. These are graceful, low-slung killing machines; silent and deadly, they are perfectly adapted to slide through the grass in search of prey. But the real masters of motorway hunting are far less secretive and much easier to see. It is now almost impossible to drive any distance without regularly passing the familiar silhouette of a motionless kestrel floating high above the roadside, on its never-ending search for prey. Kestrels are the only British birds that can truly hover for any length of time. Others can flap wildly and just about manage to hang in the air for a few seconds but kestrels are delicate, silent avian helicopters that use their unique skill to pinpoint small animals. A hunting kestrel, suspended in the air, keeps its head completely stationary so its sharp eyes can detect even the slightest movement on the ground below. When it spots a mouse, the agile falcon folds its long pointed wings and drops like a stone, grabbing the unfortunate animal with powerful talons that squeeze until life is extinguished.

In the 1950s kestrels were rapidly becoming an endangered species; newly introduced, near-lethal agricultural chemicals threatened to wipe them out completely. These were eventually banned at about the same time as the first British motorway was created – an unlikely lifeline that was grasped enthusiastically. The kestrels had a completely new, undisturbed hunting territory that was rapidly filling with mice and almost tailor-made for their talents. In just two decades the kestrel population mushroomed and went on to become amazingly successful. Their numbers grew and the enterprising falcons followed the motorway-building programme all around the country. Today there is about one pair of kestrels per linear mile of motorway. They have become so much a part of the landscape that people no longer notice them; kestrels are now the unofficial symbol of motorway wildlife.

Because of the large variety of predators circling their world, most small animals are understandably paranoid and horribly frightened of anything larger than a snail. This makes life difficult for wildlife film-makers; mice, voles and their kin disappear into the undergrowth with supernatural speed at the merest rumour of a cameraman in the vicinity. Like everyone else we only ever get occasional glimpses of these shy creatures in the wild, and they are always running rapidly away from us. We have no magic, secret technique that avoids this fear so, to get the kind of crystal clear pictures that are expected by modern audiences, television cameramen must sometimes be brutally practical and economical with reality. If my camera couldn't get close to wild mice on a verge, the mice would have to come to me. A zoologist friend was carrying out research into rodent behaviour and had several colonies of wood mice that had been bred in captivity. They were quite happy being handled by humans and were absurdly friendly. I borrowed two that were, quite frankly, both as daft as a brush. They would sit on my hand to eat and, once, even go to sleep.

These mice may have been representatives of a wild species but they were so domesticated that they would not worry about the presence of a camera or the human behind it. They had spent their entire lives

Kestrels are often the only wildlife people notice on motorways

being watched and they made perfect stars for my film. Once this initial moral barrier had been breached, there seemed little point in stopping. I couldn't possibly subject these charming animals to the rigours of a genuine motorway so I built one in my studio. Well not exactly a whole motorway, it was more of a thin slice. A road building company kindly donated a cross section of motorway, only it had been slightly scaled down to make it more manageable. The strange construction was made up of the verge and hard shoulder, together with slow, middle and part of the fast lane. It was even fitted with a crash barrier, white lines and cats' eyes. From side to side the studio motorway was almost life-size, but from one end to the other it was just three strides long. For a while I was the proud owner of the shortest motorway on earth.

This Machiavellian manipulation may shock you to the very core but is a perfectly normal technique in natural history programmes. Small mammals in the wild are so terrified of humans, it is simply impossible to get close enough to film them. The only alternative is to build a convincing set indoors and work with tame animals. TV studios all over the world have been cunningly decorated to look like hedgerows, woodlands, barley fields, sewers and almost every other conceivable habitat. We bring in nettles, drain pipes, turf, we build ponds and create artificial rain. Contrary to the old adage the camera can – and does – lie very, very convincingly. With a spot of creative lighting and good editing, the final sequence shows the secret life of a small animal, in its natural habitat, that is totally indistinguishable from reality, leaving the audience to gasp in admiration, 'how on earth did they manage to do that?' Literally thousands of wildlife films have been made using this devious approach. My stunted motorway was just another example of the imaginative and underhanded skulduggery used in television filming.

The bizarre object arrived on a huge truck and, after a Herculean struggle, was unloaded into the studio. The cat's eyes were sparkling clean, the white lines snow-white and the tarmac coal-black, warm and still sticky. It had only been laid that morning and it just looked too new. On screen it would be glaringly obvious that this tarmac had never felt the weight of a single tyre. My motorway needed to be distressed a little and I spent hours attempting to age the road surface. Broken glass was liberally sprinkled around, along with mangled cigarette ends, ring-pulls from drinks cans and even part of a frayed old fan-belt. But at the end of the day it merely looked like an untidy, brand-new motorway. After only a few days of use, real roads look battered, but mine was factory fresh. It took a while to solve this problem but I am quite happy to pass on the solution. Should any of you ever feel the need to make a new chunk of tarmac look old – simply empty the contents of a vacuum cleaner bag on top and grind it in with your feet. This instant ageing works wonders; in just a couple of hours your pristine road will look just as grey and depressing as the most well-used urban clearway.

Although the background now looked authentic there was still one vital element missing – traffic. It is the menacing, predatory presence of cars and lorries that makes the motorway wildlife story so remarkable; vehicles had to be clearly visible to remind viewers of the omnipresent threat facing animals that live on the verge. But my motorway was only as long as the average dining table, and using real cars for filming would obviously be something of a problem. It needed another illusion, this time created with a toy train set built in a long, thin oval on the 'fast lane' of the motorway.

The controls were set to run non-stop and the tiny train kept going round and round, taking just over a minute to finish one whole circuit. Twelve large torches, each a different size, were taped in pairs onto every third carriage; six had ordinary white bulbs while the other six had red bulbs. The white lights faced in one direction and the red pointed the other way. When the train was running from right to left, on the piece of track closest to the camera, only the white torches could be seen. At the end of the oval, when the train rounded the bend and went the other way, just the red pairs could be seen. The scene was completed with a generous shower of 'rain' from a watering can that soaked the tarmac.

I gently released one of the tame mice onto the grassy verge, where he sat contentedly against the background of a totally convincing motorway. Because wood mice are nocturnal, the set was deliberately kept dark; there was just one faint light aimed on the leading character of the piece. The camera started rolling and the obliging animal looked casually around before picking up the hawthorn berry I had carefully dropped in the grass just two minutes earlier. Mice hold food in their paws and nibble delicately; this one loved berries and would probably sit for thirty seconds before moving. As the film minutely recorded the mouse's eating habits every few seconds, in the background gloom, two distant and out of focus white lights would come sliding past. Simultaneously going in the other direction – and slightly further away – remote pairs of faint red lights providing a near perfect imitation of passing traffic. Because the torches were all different there was a convincing mixture in the power and size of the lights. These could easily be the headlights of any assorted stream of traffic and they were all reflected in the wet tarmac, giving an even more mixed jumble of moving red and white lights. When the film was edited we just added a convincing sound track recorded from a motorway bridge near Birmingham. Eight months later unsuspecting viewers watched a programme showing a mouse eating a berry on a motorway verge, while lights from an endless stream of vehicles tore past, accompanied by the roar and thunder of rush-hour traffic.

There is a terrible irony about the fact that, a few miles from the truncated motorway, the wild counterparts of my mice thrived and successfully conducted their lives just a few steps away from the biggest single killer of wildlife in the western world – traffic. The hedgehogs, shrews and rabbits that live on the verge are perfectly safe just as long as they don't venture out onto the tarmac. They have no margin for error: they learn to avoid traffic or they die. Strangely, though, there are some animals that do seem to be changing their core behaviour to compensate for this new threat. One of the basic nature facts taught to all schoolchildren is the idea that hedgehogs curl up into a tight ball when frightened by an enemy. The thick forest of spines is a perfect defence against the teeth of a fox or stoat, predators that specialise in taking hedgehog-sized prey. A few sharp, painful jabs in the eyes and nose soon teach hunters to keep away from these formidably armoured creatures. Over countless millennia, hedgehogs have developed a powerful instinct to curl up into a tight ball whenever danger looms. This is a wonderful strategy against a fox but somewhat less than effective when the enemy is a seventy tonne truck hurtling along the fast lane of a motorway.

Researchers have now discovered that some hedgehogs are learning to modify their response. A few of the more street-wise animals living close to fast roads are starting to differentiate between various types of danger. If an over-enthusiastic Doberman shows too much interest, they still roll up but if a tow-truck appears – they begin to run. This is not as incredibly clever as it first appears. Not all hedgehogs are the same; some are timid and hypersensitive creatures that will roll up at the drop of a hat. Others live more daringly and leave it to the last moment. The hedgehogs that curl up at the first sniff of danger will often do so in the middle of the road when they hear the first rumble of an approaching lorry. Inevitably they die under its wheels. But those that continue to walk stand a better chance of escaping. There is a theory that this is evolution in action. The genes of the dead hedgehogs die with them, so slowly the 'rapid rolling' response will become weaker. The 'walkers' however, being more likely to survive, pass on their characteristics to their offspring.

The fastest hedgehogs live longer and produce more babies. So each successive generation produces an increasingly high number of sprinters. Throughout the history of life, animals have been forced to adapt to avoid predators; today vehicles are their biggest enemy and wildlife must respond to the new threat. In this way traffic is unintentionally weeding out the slowest hedgehogs and may be effecting the very nature of the animals around us.

The logical conclusion to this hypothesis is to foresee a time when our great, great grandchildren look out on a world where hedgehogs have legs like greyhounds. Capable of accelerating from 0 to 60 mph in four seconds, they could cross the M1 faster than a Ferrari and have evolved their way out of trouble. Of course this is probably wildly inaccurate speculation but, for me at least, it is these endless possibilities that make wildlife so fascinating. The natural world never stands still; it is always moving forward and adapting. We will never fully understand wild animals, because they will always continue to change.

For the moment the theory of accelerated evolution has yet to be

proven so wildlife must cope with current reality and every year millions of animals are still killed by traffic. This is a tragedy but even death plays its part in the life of a motorway verge, which is a complex eco-system where nothing is wasted. When an animal dies on the road, its remains are absorbed back into the food chain. Corpses are a very important element in the diet of scavengers such as crows and rooks. These black strutting birds can be seen on every single motorway in the country; they spend hours each day patrolling the tarmac looking for recent casualties. They are quick to find easy meals. With effortless skill a crow can dart between maniacally racing vehicles to grab a morsel of food. When a giant lorry approaches they move at the very last moment, narrowly missing their own destruction by a fraction of a second.

The interlinked cycle of life-and-death is important to the motorway story and had to be included in the finished programme to give a balanced picture. The director asked me to find a road kill, wait until the scavengers arrived and film whatever happened next. But we were now on potentially thin ice; television audiences can sometimes be surprisingly squeamish about blood and gore so we always try to keep it to a minimum. Most animals that meet their end on the tarmac are unrecognisable after death; a completely flat rabbit or hedgehog would have been far too gruesome for most TV viewers.

To avoid a flood of irate letters and telephone complaints, I needed a rabbit that looked as if it had passed away peacefully in its sleep; there could be no suggestion of a violent death. To protect fragile audience sensibilities, I had to film an animal that didn't look too dead. If there is one thing I have learned after twenty years, it's the fact that decent rabbit corpses are impossible to find when you really need one. Suddenly the entire rabbit population of England seemed to have developed an acute road-sense and refused to go anywhere near moving traffic. There was not a single body anywhere. After two hours fruitlessly cruising the motorway system I finally realised that this was a total waste of time and a spot of lateral thinking was needed.

In Shrewsbury, the county town of Shropshire, there used to be a wonderful old-fashioned butcher's shop. It was one of those that are rapidly vanishing, a shop where the assistants would cut up the meat to order and greet every customer by name. But, most importantly of all, this shop had a licence to deal in game. Hanging in the front window, along with fresh pheasants and hunks of venison, there was always a row of unskinned rabbits suspended on stainless steel hooks. I bought the biggest on show and an hour later carefully laid the animal on a motorway verge, close to a spot where scavenger search parties regularly plied their grisly trade. By now it was almost dusk and, overhead, flocks of crows were gathering ready to fly to their tree roosts for the night. Attracting wildlife to food is a devious and well used trick known as baiting, but it only works if animals are given time to find the meal. My plan was to leave the rabbit overnight so that the crows would discover it sometime during the morning and I could film them later in the day.

When I drove back to the verge the following afternoon, the rabbit had completely disappeared. There was not a trace of blood or fur to show it had already been eaten, so it seemed likely that the corpse had been taken by a passing fox who carried it off to eat in less noisy surroundings. Wild animals seldom perform exactly to plan; setbacks like this happen everyday and the loss of a rabbit was hardly a disaster. With a mental shrug I drove back to the butcher's shop for a replacement and, later that evening, left it on the verge as an offering to the ever-hungry birds. When I returned to the motorway the next morning, the second rabbit was gone and this time I started to get annoyed.

It had rained during the night and in the soft fresh mud at the edge of the hard shoulder there were the unmistakable footprints of a big dog-fox. I followed the tracks up to a gap in the fence at the top of the verge where the animal had obviously squeezed through. A tuft of rust-red fur was caught on the wire and I could just picture him struggling to drag the rabbit through the tiny hole, before taking it into a quiet copse to eat. After two free meals this fox obviously now believed he had discovered a fast food delivery service. He didn't need to go out and hunt for mice and rats: dead rabbits were being dropped off at his doorstep. He was ready and willing to take full advantage of his good fortune. Foxes learn very quickly and this one would make a beeline for the verge every night. I had no doubt that the animal would take any bait left out on that stretch of motorway. I am a great admirer of foxes, they are bright survivors, but this one was costing me a fortune in dead rabbits and lost time. It had to be thwarted.

The butcher was mildly surprised by the third appearance of his mysterious new customer with an insatiable appetite for rabbits.

'Are you new around these parts?' He asked with barely concealed curiosity.

'I'm just passing through really,' I replied, not wanting to become too deeply involved in an explanation on the unsavoury feeding habits of crows.

'My, my. You certainly enjoy your rabbit stew, don't you. I'll have to order some more if you keep this up.'

With a wrapped rabbit under my arm I went to the camping shop next door to buy two long metal tent pegs and a wooden mallet. This particular bait was going nowhere. If the fox wanted to steal it, he had better come equipped with a pickaxe. Back on the motorway, the latest rabbit was artistically arranged on the grass next to the hard shoulder and, with the aid of the tent pegs, I made absolutely certain that no fox would walk off with this free meal without a fight. Arranging dead rabbits is another of the more unlikely skills required by modern wildlife photographers. The corpse had to look realistic; it took some time to get the position exactly right, ensuring that the tent pegs were hidden from the camera.

Until you have actually been on the receiving end, it is utterly impossible to imagine the looks of complete disbelief that appear on the faces of passing motorists as they watch a madman nail a dead rabbit to the motorway verge. Even today I can imagine a scene where drivers tell their sceptical grandchildren about the time they saw a wild-eyed man sitting on the hard shoulder torturing innocent rabbits with simple camping implements.

The police arrived within five minutes, in a storm of screeching brakes and flashing blue lights. They were well accustomed to handling irate motorists but this time they were dealing with someone armed with a mallet and tent pegs. This situation called for tact and diplomacy.

'What the bloody hell do you think you're doing?' Demanded the bigger of two awesomely large policemen.

I explained the situation to the increasingly incredulous officers, and eventually produced my official Department of Transport motorway pass. These permits are as rare as hens' teeth and obviously neither had ever seen such an object. One stayed chatting politely, keeping well out of mallet's reach, while the other went back to his car radio presumably to check my paperwork. He came back satisfied and explained that a passing lorry driver had contacted the local police headquarters on his mobile telephone and left a garbled message about a 'nutcase lying on the verge, murdering rabbits with a hammer'.

The police were finally convinced that I was harmless, but just as they were leaving one asked,

'Do you do this full time or is it just a hobby?'

'No. It's my real job.'

'So somebody actually pays you to take pictures of dead rabbits on the side of a motorway?'

'Er, well, yes.'

'It's a funny way to make a living.' He said and, after a long disbelieving stare, stepped into the police car and roared away.

5

The Way
to an Animal's Heart

Foxes may well thwart my plans at every opportunity but I cannot help admiring them. Over the centuries they have been poisoned, shot, trapped, chased by packs of specially trained dogs and yet still they survive and prosper. Although I do have to grudgingly admit that foxes occasionally take the odd chicken and goose, we shouldn't forget that, on the whole, they do us more favours than injury. Foxes are much smaller than most people think; they are closer in size to a cat rather than a dog, they look bigger because they have long legs. Stories of foxes slaughtering and devouring sheep are a foul slander: they are just not big enough for mayhem on that scale. Foxes prefer more manageable prey; they eat voles, rats and mice. Each fox munches its way through an army of rodents every year; if ever they were wiped out we would be up to our armpits in small furry mammals. These would invade our houses, eat our crops and make us rue the day foxes vanished.

Foxes probably evolved as woodland animals and were in Britain long before the first men arrived. But their opportunistic nature has allowed them to adapt to the modern, artificial world that has been moulded by humans. Foxes have the right idea, they sit back while busy *homo sapiens* reshapes the landscape; they then move in and casually learn to exploit the new surroundings. Today they can be found in mountains, farmyards, shopping malls, woodlands and housing estates. I am fascinated by their endless ingenuity and luckily publishers and book buyers share this interest. Pictures of foxes are some of the most requested wildlife photographs in Europe, which means that I have a powerful economic incentive to go out and work with some of my favourite animals. This is how all jobs should be.

But, inevitably, every silver lining has its cloud. After centuries of abuse and persecution foxes have come to fear humans, and this makes photography difficult. Foxes are bright: they recognise potential danger long before it gets close enough to pose a real threat. But, as with so many other animals, we can use this sharp intellect as a key to solve the conundrum. Foxes know exactly where danger lurks. It comes in the form of man-smell near the entrance to their den, or in the sound of baying hounds over the horizon, and they will run from the reverberating explosion of distant shotguns because each of these are familiar warning signals. However foxes have also learned to recognise the harmless features of their habitat: this easy familiarity allows us to invent a devious ruse to get close to them.

It is not only on motorways that road traffic poses a terrible danger to wildlife; cars are everywhere and even quick-witted, nimble-footed foxes are not immune to this omnipresent threat. Analysis of skeletons shows that ninety percent of urban foxes are hit by vehicles at least once during their life; most bear the scars of several encounters. To survive they must learn a degree of road-sense, they have to grasp that moving cars are to be avoided at all cost but, in the process, they also discover that stationary cars are completely harmless. Foxes, and almost every other living animal, know that these monsters are only dangerous while moving. A car with its engine off makes no noise and most of its appalling smell has vanished; it is simply another, irrelevant, part of the modern landscape.

An inoffensive parked car makes a wonderful hide where a wildlife photographer can sit while, all around, animals go about their daily lives completely unaware of the fact that they are being watched. The smell of the car also helps mask the distinctive scent of humans. The trick is finding the right place to park and that takes a bit of legwork. Foxes are creatures of habit; each has its own territory that provides food and shelter but, as this can cover more than a square mile, just knowing the foxes' boundaries is not always terribly helpful. We need to work out precisely where to set up the cameras and wait. The chances of success can be greatly improved by adapting the 'dead-rabbit' manoeuvre. In other words, we carefully pick a suitably attractive background, where a fox would look absolutely wonderful in a photograph, and then teach the animal to stand in exactly the right spot by leaving out food.

Foxes give birth in underground dens known as earths. These are built in quiet, secluded places where the vixen and cubs will be overlooked and undisturbed. They can be next to hedges, amongst tree roots or under garden sheds. The cubs are born blind and helpless: dark brown balls of fluff that are so tiny they would easily fit into the palm of my hand. At first smell is their only truly developed sense: inside the shelter of the pitch-black earth the cubs absorb the scent of their mother and siblings. For the first weeks of life they must stay within the safety of the tunnel to avoid being eaten by other predators. But quickly, nurtured by mother's rich milk, the cubs grow bigger and become intensely curious about the outside world. They first, tentatively, stick their noses out at about three weeks old. And that's literally all they do. One sharp sniff of fresh air and they dart back into the sanctuary of the cold, dark tunnel. But once freedom has been tasted, they are inexorably drawn back for more.

Adult foxes are sleek, lean and elegant but cubs lack the well-groomed panache of the parents. Adults are dog-shaped while cubs are pudding-shaped. Very young foxes have short, stubby legs and distended stomachs. They are clumsy and badly co-ordinated. Try to imagine a small balloon filled with water and fitted with four legs, then you'll have a fair idea of the average fox cub at a month old. On their first expedition outside the den, cubs waddle around exploring a small corner of their future universe. At this time they still rely exclusively on milk but once their mother starts carrying back solid food when they reach the age of about five weeks, the cubs' lives change forever.

The introduction of meat brings about a radical shift in the cubs' behaviour: they become much more aggressive and competitive. They turn into growling, biting rivals, each frantically trying to gulp down the food before the others can reach it. This opens a fracture in the fabric of family that grows with the cubs and eventually obliges each to go its separate way. But for a while, life is sweet; mother does the hunting and the cubs must wait and play. They chase each other's tails, stalk butterflies and bask in the sunshine. They screech around like manic, overwound clockwork toys; digging and chewing and jumping and fighting, they completely exhaust themselves before collapsing close to the den entrance for a few minutes and then starting the exhilarating games all over again.

Young cubs never venture far from the earth; at the first sign of danger – real or imagined, they dart underground in a swirl of legs and tails, quicker than a human eye can follow. Half the time two, or even more, cubs reach the entrance at the same time and get log-jammed. With back legs pedalling frantically two young foxes try to squeeze, side by side, down a one-cub size hole. The complete lack of progress only increases their already heightened sense of panic; they push and fight wildly in a mighty effort to escape. From inside the hole come the unmistakable sounds of biting and snarling as each cub tries to intimidate its fellow into reversing. They never do. Stones and soil fly, and the short, strong legs begin to blur as they scrabble and scramble to get inside. Then suddenly and mysteriously something gives and, like scraps of fluff sucked down a drainpipe, the cubs disappear into the hole at the speed of light.

Foxes are members of the dog family – the canids. They have a lot in common with the familiar domestic animal that retrieves thrown sticks and barks at postmen. However, for wildlife photographers, one of the most significant similarities between the two creatures are teeth. It may seem unlikely but these apparently insignificant objects are vitally important when trying to take pictures of foxes. Those who have been through the experience will know, to their cost, exactly what happens when puppies start teething. The sensation caused by erupting molars brings on a frantic desire to chew. Puppies gnaw on slippers, table legs, doormats and almost anything else that fits into their mouths. Fox cubs suffer from the same irrepressible need to chew, only their choice of objects is more restricted. When the tiny teeth buds first break through tender gums the irritation drives young foxes to distraction. They gnaw roots, sticks, each other and even stones to soothe the constant soreness. Within a few days the area around the earth entrance is reduced to a rubbish tip. Every visible object is covered with bite-marks and splinters of wood are scattered in all directions. This coincides with the cubs' first crude attempts at digging and soon the young foxes have excavated a fine collection of experimental holes, preparing for the time when they will dig for worms or their own breeding dens. There may also be a few exhausted bones lying about, marking the remains of earlier meals brought back by mother. The cubs' playground quickly takes on the appearance of a battlefield.

With a little time and patience, photography near the earth is not impossible. But it is a total waste a time. We can easily take pictures of both mother and cubs but they are standing in a landscape that appears to have been trampled by a herd of rampaging rhinos. A wildlife photograph can be made or broken by the background; quite often it is the most important element of the picture and must be chosen carefully. If a fox is inconsiderate enough to stand in the wrong spot we must occasionally persuade it to move somewhere more photogenic by using bait. It is now absolutely essential to recall the pine marten philosophy, ie. don't be tempted to leave out food that the animal eats normally. It needs a treat, something special that is worth the effort of moving. And if there's one thing that foxes love above all else – it's chocolate. They will kill for

Cadbury's Dairy Milk.

When the fox earth is in the centre of a bombsite and just around the corner is a bank of beautiful wild flowers, we teach it to go from one to the other by leaving out a trail of chocolate drops. Every evening for a week tiny squares of chocolate are left in an unmistakable line leading from the earth to the flowers. When the foxes come out of the den, they spend a few minutes scratching and stretching; they then bite each other for a while just to pass the time, and only then do they lower their noses to the ground to begin the search for food. The first chocolate drop is discovered by accident, the next one in line might be overlooked and the fox may then discover another halfway down the trail. But foxes are quick to learn. The trail of chocolate is left out in the same place every day and by the fifth night they know precisely where to find it and come out like vacuum cleaners, eagerly sucking up chocolate along a path that leads straight to the bank of flowers. The fox must now be persuaded to stand, while I take pictures. This involves yet more chocolate, but this time used with subtlety. It's tempting to opt for quantity so that the animal will stand for a long time to eat. But a whole bar lying on the ground would probably be picked up immediately and carried back to the den; the fox wouldn't even slow down to collect her meal.

To concentrate the action in one spot, the chocolate must first be left in a freezer overnight and, wrapped in newspaper, taken to the earth still frozen. This brings me to the most important gadget in the arsenal of a fox photographer - a nutmeg grater. With this handy kitchen implement the rock-hard chocolate is soon reduced to a pile of shavings which are scattered in the grass in front of the flowers. The tiny chocolate specks quickly melt and give out a rich scent that will, quite literally, make a fox's mouth water at twenty metres. When the fox follows the familiar trail and finds the treasure trove of grated chocolate, she can't pick it up and run. She must stand still and delicately lick up the heavenly snack, while posing against a wonderful background of wild flowers. Of course, jelly babies and liquorice allsorts would do the job just as well. But the pink, orange and blue blobs in the grass would give the game away. Chocolate is perfect because, hidden amongst the soil, leaves and twigs, the tiny brown flecks are camouflaged and completely invisible to the watching camera.

This is where a car comes in useful. The background isn't chosen just because of its aesthetic qualities; it has to be accessible. With foxes I always try to find a spot which can be reached by car. While they would be extremely suspicious of a conventional canvas hide, a car parked a hundred metres away is simply irrelevant. The beauty of this approach is that I know exactly where the fox will stand. The camera can be set up on a tripod close to the bait, covered by branches, and operated by remote control. I can sit comfortably in the car, sipping coffee and nibbling the remains of the frozen chocolate.

When the fox appears and starts eagerly sucking up the sweet, hidden bait, the camera is already focused precisely on the right spot. The only problem is that the fox's nose is lowered immediately in an anxious bid to poke about in the grass to reach the chocolate. Ideally I want a photograph with the animal's head held high, not masked by the undergrowth. So I blow the fox a kiss, a sharp squeaky kiss that sounds like the alarm call of a rabbit. No fox can ever ignore this tantalising noise and like a jack-in-the-box its head springs up and looks directly at the source of the sound. A quick press of a button on the remote control and the distant camera takes five pictures in a second. Instead of photographing the fox in front of a pile of excavated earth and horribly mutilated branches, these photographs show a fox standing against a glorious bank of wild flowers. And all it takes is a family sized bar of chocolate.

Wildlife photography has been with us for almost 150 years. From the moment the first primitive cameras were made, we have tried to take pictures of animals. In the mid-nineteenth century early portraits of native wildlife were greeted with huge interest and acclaim. They may have been out of focus blobs, in grainy black-and-white, but they were the beginning of a new artform. Some psychologists have suggested that wildlife photography has become a replacement for hunting. Now that most us get our food hygienically wrapped from a supermarket, there is no need to go out into the wilds and stalk animals. But many people think that there is a real need for humans to have direct contact with the natural world. Wildlife photography requires similar skills to hunting: the cameraman has to pit his wits against the acute senses of an animal.

He must know how to read tracks and understand the countryside to get anywhere near his quarry. And, in the end, there is the enormously important advantage that nothing gets hurt.

Wildlife photography has become a hugely popular hobby with literally millions of followers travelling the world every year in search of new subjects. Unfortunately that means that there are now an awful lot of photographs around and it is getting ever more difficult to take a picture that is sufficiently new and interesting to grab the attention of the viewer. Like most aspiring photographers, my early ambition was to get really close, to produce images where the animal filled the picture frame. I wanted to see every feather, every eyelash, details that were impossible to spot using my own eyesight. I can now see that this was an enormous mistake. I spent months getting close enough to take pictures where the animal occupied ninety percent of the picture and the results were deadly dull; I can't escape from the absurd idea that they were passport photographs. The poor creatures looked stuffed. The photographs had no interest, no atmosphere or humour – they simply lacked any sense of life. This was to be a vitally important lesson that was to shape my work for many years to come.

Wildlife photography today is a very sophisticated business. Publishers demand pictures that show not only what the animal looks like but also give an idea of where and how it lives. They want action, drama and a story. Today before ever picking up a camera, I sit down to work out exactly what to show in the picture – and then devise a way to achieve it. One of my very earliest commissions was to write a series of articles on garden wildlife for a children's magazine: the editor wanted to publish a guide to the animals that entered a typical British domestic garden.

To illustrate the text, amongst the pictures of foxes and hedgehogs, there had to be some interesting images of birds. I didn't want them just sitting on a branch; they needed to look a bit more dynamic – ideally in a recognisable garden setting. I quickly scanned a heap of gardening magazines looking for ideas for pictures and eventually, in a readers' letters page, there it was. Someone had written to advocate the joys of creating a wildlife garden, they 'even enjoyed the daily sight of great tits struggling to open the milk bottles to reach their morning drink'. This was a perfect inspiration. A common garden bird, in an obvious garden setting – and it could be photographed doing something interesting.

I spent the next few days trying to locate suitably talented great tits. Opening milk bottles is not an instinctive skill; great tits have not spent millions of years evolving the ability to tear off rounded sheets of aluminium. They are, by nature, insect eaters that busily explore nooks and crannies looking for creepy-crawlies. Opening milk bottles is a recent variation that not all have learned; it seems to be cultural and can be found in some areas but is completely missing from others. Most great tits live in rural woodlands but the majority of specialist bottle burglars are found in built-up areas where milk is more likely to be delivered. This brand of thievery is largely a suburban phenomenon. Eventually, through the local wildlife grapevine, I tracked down a garden where great tits had been opening milk bottles for several years.

I've always found that most people are only too happy to oblige when 'their' animals are needed by wildlife photographers, especially when the results will be published in magazines and seen all over the country. I telephoned to explain my quest and was invited round the next day to see if the site was suitable. Mr Harding, who owned the house, was a very keen gardener and was, understandably, very proud of the fact that flowers, vegetables and birds thrived alongside each other.

'These birds have been pinching milk every day, summer and winter, since we moved in', he explained. 'I don't begrudge them a teaspoon of cream, if they keep the caterpillars off my cabbages.'

This was a man after my own heart: I've always believed that gardens shouldn't be just for the benefit of humans. A garden without wildlife is strangely sterile and sad.

It was a huge redbrick Victorian house, with a doorstep made of slate which stuck out a long way from the front door. The step was overlooked by the dining room window and this was an ideal place to set up a camera. From here I would be able to see any bird that came down to take the milk.

Mr Harding explained, 'The milkman comes about nine o'clock, when we're both out to work. It sits out on the doorstep until lunchtime, when the wife comes back. So the birds have plenty of time to take what they want.'

There was just one slight hitch: the front door faced west and in the morning, when the milk arrived, the sun was on the other side of the house leaving the step in deep shadow. I needed a bit more light and arranged to come back the next afternoon when the sun had moved round.

On my way to their house the following day I stopped at a supermarket to buy two pints of milk. Mrs Harding was home when I arrived.

'The birds have already had some breakfast this morning,' she said, showing me a bottle with a ripped aluminium lid and the top layer of cream missing.

I opened the dining room window slightly, slid my telephoto lens through the gap and closed the thick velvet curtains around the camera. From inside the house, through the lens, I could clearly see the doorstep. The birds on the outside could only see a pair of closed green curtains.

Once the camera was set up I leant out of the door, put my two milk bottles on the step, crept quickly into the house and sat behind the curtains. A great tit landed on the doorstep almost immediately, pecked idly at a clump of bedraggled weeds by the front door and then flew off to a nearby lilac tree where, presumably, the pickings were more promising. As the first great tit left another dropped onto the lawn, next to the step and started probing the short grass for insects. I sat glued to the camera all afternoon, while great tits and their cousins, blue tits and coal tits, flitted about the garden, totally ignoring the proffered milk. Although there would only be one pair of great tits living in this small territory, I counted twenty-three occasions when they came close to the bottles. And not once did they show even a tiny spark of interest in the meal.

Mr Harding came in from work at about six o'clock. He stuck his head around the dining room door and hissed, 'Any luck?'

'No', I muttered grumpily, 'not a sausage. The birds have been around all day. They even landed next to the bottles. But they just didn't seem to want any milk.'

'Well isn't that strange,' mused Mr Harding, 'they're keen enough every other day. Maybe they're frightened of you.'

I have to admit that this thought had already crossed my mind; the curtains were closed around my camera lens and, from the garden, it was impossible to see me skulking behind. But animals have a sixth sense about humans and it could be that the great tits were aware of being watched. I would have to be more careful next time.

The following day I crept around like a cat on hot coals, showing myself long enough to gently lower two bottles onto the doorstep. But the results were exactly the same. The birds appeared, they strolled about the lawn and even perched on the step – but they took absolutely no notice of the milk.

It was time to rethink the problem. The birds were in the garden and the milk was within their reach but the two just wouldn't come together. There must be something I hadn't considered. Then it came to me. These were the wrong milk bottles; birds can sometimes be very fussy when it comes to food. My milk came from a supermarket, in bottles that were a different shape to those delivered by the milkman. It could be that the birds didn't recognise that my milk could provide a meal. That was easily solved; I found a shop that sold identical bottles and left those on the step. These were also totally ignored.

As I watched the inscrutably uncooperative birds flit about the garden it occurred to me that perhaps these were unusually moderate great tits who were trying to limit their cholesterol intake. Maybe they would only feed once a day and my second helping was more than they wanted or needed. This was a long shot I'll grant, but the few remaining options were beginning to slip through my fingers. The great tits' rations obviously had to be cut, to make them lean and keen. The next day, with long-suffering patience, the Hardings agreed to cancel their milk on the strict understanding that I would bring in supplies at lunchtime.

The following afternoon, once the camera was ready, the bottles were discreetly slipped onto the doorstep before I dashed inside the house. This was the first milk of the day and a great tit came down immediately. It landed on an ailing rosebush next to the door and started picking invisible insects from the thorny stem. After a few seconds the bird looked around then flew over the hedge at the edge of the garden and disappeared. I was completely stumped: what did these infernal birds want? They had the right bottles, in the right place, they hadn't already gorged themselves but still they would not behave. Could it be that they had developed an intolerance to dairy products overnight? Frustration is a frequent and familiar emotion in wildlife photography; it was like gazing at an immensely complex jigsaw puzzle. I had the final picture in mind, all the elements were in front of me but they couldn't be fitted together in a way that worked.

Suddenly a light dawned with blinding clarity. I grabbed two bottles, took them out of the house, down the garden path and out of the gate. I walked to my car and loitered suspiciously for five minutes, before opening the driver's door and slamming it noisily. Walking back to the house, I clanked the bottles together and, as loud as possible, whistled a bright, tuneless melody. I deliberately crashed the bottles down onto the step and dived in through the front door. Fifteen seconds later, as I watched through a crack in the curtains, a great tit landed on the bottle, speared the thin aluminium lid and prized it open with a vicious twist of its neck. The tiny black and white head disappeared deep into the open bottle and the bird took a long drink of thick, fresh cream. In less than a minute I finished a whole roll of film. The pictures all worked perfectly but they had certainly been earned the hard way.

Great tits may be bright, but these had not understood the whole sequence of events. Birds probably first started stealing milk during the Second World War. In those days resources were stretched; doorstep milk deliveries were hardly a high priority and the glass – and factories – were needed for more vital products. For a while milk was packaged and delivered in flimsy cardboard containers which really needed to be decanted immediately into a jug. If the thin cartons were left for any length of time, they simply disintegrated. But, as now, milk often sat on the doorstep for a while before being taken in and, inevitably, the boxes split open. All over the country, birds were presented with gaping holes full of a previously unattainable food. This was more than sixty years ago, in a time long before our own health conscious days, when milk was rich and bursting with full-fat cream. Fat is one of the most important elements in the diet of a wild animal, it provides almost pure protein and helps them survive the rigours of winter. The birds took to it with gusto and learned to check the doorstep every day.

After the war, when life started to return to normal, glass bottles made a reappearance. For some birds this marked the end of the halcyon days. The robins, blackbirds and sparrows that could easily drink from an open cardboard box just weren't physically equipped to wrestle with an aluminium foil top fitted onto a tall glass tube. Only the agile, tenacious tits could make the adjustment. They had become accustomed to taking this luxurious food every morning and, on the day when the card boxes were abandoned and replaced, they simply turned their attention to the bottles. The thin, soft metal was soon breached and the birds resumed their lucrative pilfering. This behaviour has since been passed on to to successive generations but they have only learned to understand part of the process.

'You mean to tell me', said an incredulous Mr Harding, 'that the birds didn't recognise milk if it appeared in the middle of the day?'

'That's right,' I explained equally amazed, 'the great tits know that the milkman brings milk. They hear the whistling and the sound of bottles clanking together; they know that's the signal announcing that breakfast is served. But without those noises, they don't seem to recognise the milk bottles themselves. It's incredible.'

This strangely distorted perception of milk seemed absurd and extremely unlikely, so I tried the same test the next day. The bottles were quietly slid onto the step – with no noise or fanfare – and the birds took no notice whatsoever. When the bottles were 'delivered' to a loud accompaniment of whistling and clanking, the great tits came down to feed in a matter of seconds. They really did need the stimulus of milkman noises to make them look for their luxurious drink. Even while writing this, I realise that, in the very near future, people will go out of their way to tell me that 'their' great tits don't need this wake up call. They will eagerly report that birds in their garden will take milk at any time and in any place, in total silence or against a cacophony of nearby road-drills or a full chorus from Handel's Messiah. And I am absolutely certain that they will be telling the gospel truth. That's one of the big problems with wild animals, they're all different. I may have accidentally chosen the only great tits in the country that need audible signals before eating. They could well be unique, but they were all I had and it was their behaviour that dictated my own.

Having solved this surreal problem with finesse and insight, I was impossibly pleased with myself. When Mrs Harding came home I proudly demonstrated the test for a third time, with the same result. She was suitably impressed with the performance and watched with amazement as the birds came back when they heard the 'milkman'.

'I suppose you've just got to know how animals think in your job,' she said.

'Well, it's just practice and time really.' I replied, obviously being modest and self-deprecating.

'No. No. It's amazing. You really have to think like an animal. You must be a complete bird brain to have worked that out.'

6

The Real Bird-Brains

The intellectual capacity of an animal is a potential thorn in the side of anyone who works with wildlife. Outsiders always assume that my job is dominated by the degree of ferocity displayed by the animal in front of the camera. Let's be honest from the start and admit that this is a vitally important consideration, to be ignored at the risk of life and limb. But the root cause of the real problems and frustration is much more subtle. It all goes back to the animal's brain, its IQ, its perception of the world around. The hidden, mysterious thought processes that dictate an animal's actions ultimately control its reactions to my presence. How a creature thinks is the single biggest barrier that thwarts most of my attempts to study it. And, sad as it may seem, the truth is that brain cells have not been fairly distributed between species. Some animals have minds as sharp as a razor; they are quick and observant, not easily fooled and real pigs to handle. Others are mind-bogglingly dim and appear to have no real cerebral capacity whatsoever. These may be frustrating but at least they are a piece of cake to trick.

The highbrow giants of the bird world belong mainly to two families – crows and parrots. Both of these are bright, inventive and quick to spot an opportunity. They are also suspicious and resourceful in every sense. As I mentioned earlier, photography from a hide works only because most birds have completely failed to master the art of counting. Well, I did not tell the whole story, because not all birds are quite so intellectually challenged. A very small number have pushed forward the boundaries of avian talent and have started to become numerate.

This poses a new set of problems, perfectly illustrated by ravens. These are the biggest member of the crow family; they usually live in wild, windswept places far from towns and cities. Although – like every other species – the ravens' brainpower varies between individuals, they are all remarkably clever. But the skill that separates ravens from most other birds is that of counting. Some particularly gifted ravens can count as high as nine. This was discovered by researchers in laboratories who set about devising fiendish tests to measure animal intelligence. To cut a long story short, this sort of project is usually based on a reward system. If the bird solves the problem, it is given food. But I hasten to add that particularly thick birds are not starved, they just get their food at the end. One test required birds to peck a coloured square to make food appear down a chute. Most species of birds quickly learned to peck the square, but they did it either once or continuously. There was no sign of counting.

At first the birds were fed if the square was touched once or many times, but then the rules were changed. Food would only appear if the target was pecked the right number of times. The vast majority of birds got completely lost at this point. If food wasn't produced by the first peck, they stabbed at the square wildly and when that didn't work, they lost interest, retired into a corner and sulked.

The crow family, particularly ravens, proved that they could learn to peck the square an exact number of times to be rewarded with food. But they could only achieve this up to nine. Due to some strange quirk of evolution a raven's brain cannot cope with double figures. It is essential to remember this snippet of raven psychology when trying to photograph them in the wild. If a species has learned the basics of counting, hide photography becomes much more complicated. The time-honoured two-in, one-out trick just won't work. Once a hide is built near the nest and both birds are happy with its presence, there is absolutely no point in a cameraman taking along just one other person to see him inside. As the humans approach, the watchful ravens will take to the air, alight on a distant branch and carefully scrutinise every movement. Normally as one person enters the hide and the other leaves, most birds would be satisfied that the danger has passed. But not a raven. These wily old birds have no trouble telling the difference between one human and two. While a dim-witted robin would be fooled by this ploy the ravens will remain sceptical. Unmoving on their perch, they would simply watch the single figure disappear over the horizon while thinking to themselves 'there's still one down there somewhere.'

To solve this dilemma, we really must mentally raise our hats to thank the patient diligence of those long-ago researchers: they gave wildlife photographers the critical clue that finally helps trick the ravens' mighty brain. But we cannot do it alone. The first time I worked with ravens was at a nest built on a rocky outcrop on Dartmoor. As ravens are suspicious birds, it took more than a week to move the hide close to the nest. It was first built about fifteen metres away and each day was edged a little closer to the site. Eventually the hide was balanced on a narrow shelf of rock overlooking the giant stack of twigs and branches that formed the birds' nest.

I always like to move hides early in the morning, just after dawn when there is no-one around to see what is going to happen. The hide – and nest – need to stay concealed from prying human eyes, to protect both the ravens and the photography. The hide reached its final spot at six o'clock in the morning, leaving me plenty of time to drive to a nearby primary school where I had been asked to give a talk about local wildlife.

Young children usually love this kind of event; it makes a break from their normal work. They see someone new and for an hour the classroom is in darkness, so they can get up to all kind of mischief without being seen. Against a background of whispering and giggling I showed slides of badgers, foxes and owls and, on the whole, for eight-year olds they were pretty well behaved. At the end I asked if anyone had any questions, already knowing what to expect. Young children always seem to want to know about extremes and are particularly fascinated with danger and size. They never run short of questions – no matter how far-removed from the subject in hand.

'What's the biggest animal you've ever seen?'

'Can you swim faster than a shark?'

'What's the most dangerous animal you've ever photographed?'

'What's the biggest animal you'd like to photograph?'

'What's the biggest animal your friends have photographed?'

'Could a gorilla kill a polar bear?'

This kind of question session usually ends with an odd non-sequitur. On this particular day a little chap sat at the front with his hand straining upwards. I pointed his way and he piped up with pride, 'I've got a hamster.'

This is the inevitable stage I have come to dread in primary schools, because from that point on the questions disappear and are replaced with a never-ending string of statements along the lines of

'I've got a cat.'

'My pig's just had puppies.'

'My brother saw a squirrel last year.'

'When I grow up I'm going to Australia to catch kangaroos.'

To be honest I have never really known how to respond to these declarations, apart from smiling weakly and mouthing an appallingly bland reply such as 'that's nice'. At the first mention of hamsters or any other domestic pet, I have learned to swiftly hand the proceedings over to the teacher, who presumably faces this harrowing experience on a daily basis. This time the teacher herself had a question:

'What are you working on at the moment?'

Relieved to be let off the hook I explained about the ravens and how their intelligence and counting ability made them so difficult to approach. Sometimes children amaze me. Sixty seconds earlier these miniature inquisitors were regaling me with a long list of all the animals that have ever been encountered by their endless circle of friends and family. Yet the next moment they instantly grasp an abstract and sophisticated issue of animal behaviour. The entire class got the point immediately. In a few minutes they were giggling and writhing with delight at the thought that birds could be fooled with simple numbers that they themselves had mastered several years earlier. Suddenly the teacher was inspired. She stood and shouted:

'Children – quiet now. We've had a lovely time this morning. You've all enjoyed seeing the animal photographs, now who would like to do something to help Mr Leach?'

The entire class bellowed 'Yeeessss. Meeeeeee.'

So, after checking with their parents, two days later I borrowed a coach load of children. With the promise of some raven photographs to decorate their classroom two slightly bemused teachers, a ramshackle school bus and the thirty-six children inside arrived at a lay-by in a remote Dartmoor lane. This was rural Devon and most children lived a fair distance from school; they made the journey every day by bus. It was half-past eight in the morning and the last child had been collected, but this time they were diverted from the well-travelled route.

The children thought it was a hoot: instead of arriving at school at nine o'clock, they were asked to wander across the moorland for half an hour. There was no work to do, no drawing, no cross-country running, they just had to walk. It was a gloriously sunny, windless day. Clambering off the bus, the children were not quite sure what was expected of them but trudging over the heather and bracken, they soon got into the swing of things. This was far better than maths and they were allowed – even encouraged – to make a noise. I lead the way across the moor, carrying a rucksack full of camera equipment, together with enough coffee and sandwiches to last the day. As the unlikely, untidy group hiked eagerly towards the distant cliff-face where my hide had been built four days earlier, I actually wanted them to be noisy. The ravens needed to know exactly what was happening, they had to see humans come and then go if the deception was to succeed.

As the children scrabbled and tumbled closer to the nest site, the ravens magically appeared in the sky, producing their unmistakable dissonant, reverberating *cronks* that echoed around the landscape. They wheeled around watching the tiny, squealing invaders swarm around the base of the rocky outcrop that supported their massive nesting platform. Doing my finest impression of a cat burglar, I discreetly disappeared behind the rocks to hide from the scrutinous gaze of ravens patrolling above. The disturbance had to be kept as short as possible, I needed to get into the hide quickly. My mountaineering skills verge on the non-existent but fortunately this was more of a scramble than a climb. A few minutes later I slid into the canvas hide and hung a white handkerchief from a viewing panel in the side. This was the pre-arranged signal to tell the teachers that it was time for the decoy party to leave. From safe inside my hidden lair I could clearly hear the unmistakable yell of a teacher trying hard to control a group of uncontrollable children.

'It's time to go now children. We'll walk back the way we came; don't pick up anything nasty from the ground and don't make any noise.'

That was exactly what I didn't want. The ravens needed to watch and hear the children disappear, they had to realise that the potential threat had vanished and it was safe to return to the cliff. I needn't have worried. Following the stern warning from their teacher, the group of cute eight-year olds set off across the moor with the stealth and secrecy of a victorious, drunken football crowd. The ravens didn't really have to be anywhere near to know what was happening. The children were away from the confinement of school, this was a real adventure and the sound of their high spirits would have caught the attention of any living creature within the boundaries of the National Park. Like the diminishing aftershock of an earthquake the high-pitched cacophony gradually faded as the children climbed into the bus and drove back to normality. Five minutes later the first raven returned. These birds may be bright, they can even count up to nine, but not even the most gifted raven can tell the difference between thirty-nine people and thirty-eight people. They had seen a large group of humans approach the cliff and they had seen a large group depart, but they didn't realise that one was still there, lurking inside a small canvas box to watch their every movement. They were convinced that it was safe to return.

At close range ravens are huge: they always seem small in the sky because they keep so high above the earth. It was only when the giant black bird dropped from the air and perched almost within touching distance that I appreciated just how massive a raven can be. In overcast light their plumage looks coal black, but in that brilliant morning sunshine the feathers glowed with a green iridescence that made the creature appear to take on the mantle and characteristics of the mystical role it once held in ancient Norse mythology.

Odin, Father of All the Gods, was known amongst other things as *Hrafnagud* – the raven god. Legends say that he kept a raven on each shoulder; these were regularly sent out to patrol the skies on spying missions. The keen-eyed birds collected snippets of information about the outside world, which they brought back and whispered into Odin's ear. Although ravens are omnivores with a healthy appetite for a huge variety of foods, they are particularly partial to carrion. This taste was easy to satisfy in the Viking world of a thousand years ago, a time when murder and mayhem was a way of life for many humans. The quick-witted ravens profited from Man's barbarous activities and probably learned to follow the sound of fighting. Like sombre-clad vultures they regularly haunted battlefields to gorge themselves on the bloody remains of war.

Inevitably, in superstitious medieval minds, ravens became inextricably linked with death and they certainly looked the part. Their black, forbidding appearance helped encourage the association with dark forces and the supernatural. Some cultures believed that a raven carried the power of death and dealt it out, casually and randomly, to the watchers below. Other civilisations thought that ravens were the vessels of evil human souls, people whose actions on earth were so reprehensible that they were forever doomed to search the skies in the form of giant, black carrion eating birds.

The unfortunate raven has always been portrayed in a poor light and, sitting in my tiny canvas eyrie, I found it impossible to understand the

At close quarters, ravens are huge: about the size of a small terrier

prejudice. It had taken a complex scheme and the help of thirty-eight people to get me into the hide, so I already had a healthy respect for these birds. There were four chicks in the nest and when the first parent returned they all began clamouring for food. Ravens have enormously powerful beaks that are frequently used as efficient weapons to kill smaller prey. The bird in front of me carried a gruesome, unidentifiable chunk of gore. Using a beak that was strongly reminiscent of a pickaxe, the raven delicately pulled off tiny morsels to give to each chick in turn. From that moment on ravens became a special favourite of mine. They are fascinating in so many ways. They are one of the longest living birds in the world, they are bright, powerful and live in some of the most beautiful, wild countryside in Britain. How could anyone not exult in the existence of the mystical raven?

Ravens always strike me as the academics of the bird world. They are certainly very bright but, for some irrational reason, I've always suspected that they only apply their intelligence to worthy causes. Other members of the family are a little more street-wise and crafty. For me at least the unchallenged mastermind of the British skies is the magpie, a smaller cousin of the raven. They are smart, strutting, movers-and-shakers that know how to get what they want. They have also learned to use their brains imaginatively. If the powerful, awesome raven was the symbol of Odin, I've long thought that magpies should be associated with Loki, the 'mischief maker'. This Nordic god was clever and cunning, a deity that was never to be fully trusted.

Hides are wonderfully useful for watching birds at close range but they can also be signposts advertising food, for those that know how to read the clues. Most photographers prefer to work in quiet surroundings, away from the disturbance of humans. Public parks and gardens are too busy; wildlife is either driven away or very wary. It is much better to work on private land, where hides remain unnoticed and untroubled. But this intensive activity sometimes means that the photography is concentrated in one small area and can produce its own problems. A colleague was once working on a small estate in Wales, taking photographs for a new book on woodland birds. After about a week he noticed that an unusually high number of nests were being raided. Eggs and chicks are taken every year by woodpeckers, squirrels, cats and other opportunistic scavengers but this usually only accounts for only a small percentage of nests. However that spring almost every nest was being robbed. At first small boys from the local village were suspected of the crime. Speaking as someone who used to be one, I know that this is the first conclusion arrived at by most adults whenever anything goes wrong. A trap was set to catch the culprits. The photographer put up a hide in the middle of a field, nowhere near a nest, he then climbed a tree to sit and watch with a pair of binoculars.

Within a few minutes a magpie landed close to the hide and began to walk in ever increasing circles around it. This canny creature had discovered that a hide announced the presence of a nest and, if it looked hard enough, close by he would find a free meal. This is breathtakingly bright. Most magpies have no experince of hides. Green canvas boxes are hardly a normal part of the countryside and it is very likely that none had ever been used on that estate during the magpie's relatively short life. Yet this animal had noticed the hide, investigated it, discovered the food and intellectually made the connection between the sight of a small camouflaged tent and the existence of an easy snack. It was an incredibly clever deduction for a bird. It also signalled the end of photography in the area. Any future hide would be the kiss of death for the nearby nest. The photographer packed up and moved on to pastures new where the birds were less enterprising.

The magpies' inventive brain is certainly a great help in its battle for survival but, just as in humans, intelligence in birds can produce some very strange behaviour. Like all members of the corvid family, magpies are deeply suspicious; they seem to have an almost infallible preternatural sense that warns them of impending danger. This makes them one of the most challenging of all birds to photograph at close range.

For decades bird photography was based around nests for the simple and practical reason that, when they have chicks to feed, birds become predictable. For most of the year birds are almost impossible to pinpoint; they move around looking for food, at the mercy of the elements. But for a short time in the spring they have a focal point, a single spot to which they will continually return. This gives a cameraman an exact position to set up his equipment. With patience and knowledge nest photography is not a difficult task, but now it has been overdone. In the decades between 1900 and 1960 every British bird was photographed *ad nauseam* at the nest. There is a European photograph mountain of every resident species. Every bird, that is, except the magpie. There are two insuperable problems with this creature. First of all their nest is more like a fortress than a nursery. Magpies create huge domed structures, built of twigs and mud, usually in the centre of a dense, savagely spined bush such as blackthorn or hawthorn. The construction is cleverly woven into the branches, until it is almost an integral part of the tree. They are diabolically well hidden. Even if the nest is found, the position and design make it virtually impossible to see clearly. But that particular difficulty pales into insignificance when compared to the magpies' tendency to neophobia. They are very wary of new objects, especially when they appear anywhere near a nest. The magpie's natural suspicion turns to rabid paranoia if a hide is built almost anywhere within the visible horizon. Magpies have rarely been photographed anywhere near their nest and they are one of the most elusive subjects for many cameramen.

For more than ten years I tried occasionally to take pictures of magpies, but my attempts were only half-hearted because of the magpies' notorious reputation. The difficulties of nest photography were so daunting that I stuck to trying to find them feeding. But even this was awkward. While most other birds will eventually come down to food specially left out to attract them, magpies always seem to know when a human is nearby, no matter how well hidden he may be. After a decade I could proudly boast three photographs of wild magpies.

Late one evening the telephone went and an unknown voice enquired,

'Are you … er … the wildlife photographer?'

'That's right. Yes.' I replied, trying to sound efficient and businesslike. This was usually how people contacted me to book a talk for a camera club or Round Table.

'Would you like to photograph a magpie?'

'What!'

'A magpie. Would you like to photograph a magpie? I've got one here. It's tame. Daft as a brush. Do you want to take some pictures?'

It was after nine o'clock and already dark, otherwise I would have grabbed my camera bag and gone round there and then.

'Yes please. I'd love to. How about first thing in the morning?'

I arranged to visit the miraculous bird the next day and received very precise directions from the lady who introduced herself as Mrs Hart. I went to bed that night and dreamt of thrilling magpie photographs. Pictures that would send shivers of delight down the backbones of publishers everywhere. If only it was always this easy.

I arrived at the house, exactly on time, clutching a stuffed camera bag and tripod. An elderly lady opened the door; she was still in a dressing gown and very excited. Without even saying hello she launched into a breathless explanation, made up of very short sentences delivered in a rapid machine-gun technique that I found vaguely unsettling.

'The magpie is in the garden. It's been here since Saturday. It's very tame – it's very strange. It has odd habits. Come in. Have a look.'

We went around the side of her house, a perfectly ordinary semi on a housing estate in Shrewsbury. As we got to the garden she whistled and bellowed, with a clarity and power that was amazing coming from her tiny frame.

'Maggie. Mag, mag, mag, mag, Maggieeeee…'

I've since discovered the apparent existence of a cast-iron rule, dictating that every tame or captive magpie must be known as 'Maggie'.

Within a few seconds the bird landed delicately on a fence at the far end of the lawn. As always I was struck by the magpie's immaculate appearance. They are small birds, with long sweeping tails. While ravens wear an aura of mystique and foreboding, magpies positively radiate a quick and lively intellect. This one sat on the wooden fence and watched me carefully, rapidly weaving his head from side to side, in a sharp staccato examination. I lifted the camera and in less than a minute managed to get more magpie photographs than during the whole of the previous ten years put together. The magpie watched me for a while and then suddenly dropped onto the lawn and starting picking buttercups. I was truly stunned. Magpies are rough, tough scavengers. They can aggressively hold their ground in a full-blooded scrap with other birds. Magpies think on their feet, are quick to spot an opportunity, they are sceptical and cunning but, to the best of my knowledge, they have never been known as flower arrangers.

I was absolutely spellbound. Magpies don't eat buttercups, it was early September and the nesting season was long gone, so the bird had no need to collect bedding. I couldn't even begin to guess what the bird was doing.

Magpie armed with a buttercup

Just then a distant, insistent bell sounded from the house.

'Must go. Telephone.'

She walked into the house with a chopping, military stride that echoed her clipped speech. I was left alone in the garden with the eccentric magpie. By now the bird had gathered a small posy. Intriguingly he was only collecting buttercups. The lawn grass was long and home to a respectable display of daisies, self-heal and dandelions. But these were ignored. This magpie was a buttercup specialist. Having collected about fifteen small flowers he stopped and looked at me. Small birds, like robins, have feet that don't operate independently, they are always used together. Their feet leave the ground together and they land together, producing a distinctive hopping, bouncing movement. Magpies walk more like a human, one foot at a time. With an unhurried long-legged stride the bird strolled over and *thwack*, without a pause and with effortless precision he wedged the small bouquet of flowers into my left shoe, filling the imperceptible gap between flesh and leather. Sixty seconds later he was back with another posy which was jammed into my right shoe.

The extent of this magpie's outlandish behaviour didn't stop at an unexpected interest in horticulture. The misguided creature had completely lost its innate fear of humans, if indeed it ever had any. When it came back for the third time, the wonderful bird landed on my hip. Well, landed is probably too strong a word. Human hips are not ideally designed to act as a perch. The magpie tried to land on a vertical surface and performed a high-speed tap dance on my trousers. It's feet were slipping and sliding, like a child trying to climb up a highly polished slide. Wings helped of course; the tiny scrabbling feet and frantically flapping wings kept the magpie in position long enough for the bird to thrust a neat garland of buttercups deep into my pocket. This accomplished, he dropped to the lawn, collected more flowers and those too disappeared into a pocket. Even in my bewildered state, I could begin to see method in his madness. There were two apparent rules. Every gap, no matter how small, must be filled with buttercups, and no gap is ever to be filled twice. The magpie was working heroically to achieve his ambition.

Over the next five minutes he packed buttercups into my back pocket, belt loops, in the gaps between the buttons of my shirt and every other available aperture within view. I soon felt like a Victorian Valentine card, completely bedecked with flowers. After ten minutes of creative botany, the industrious bird finally exhausted the buttercup population of the lawn. He nimbly hopped onto the fence and vanished into the greenery of the garden next door. Just then Mrs Hart came marching along the garden path.

'Sorry about that. Phone call.'

She took a single glance at my newly-acquired ornamentation and muttered without surprise,

'Ah. You've met Maggie then.'

She went on to explain the few facts known about this extraordinary bird. Maggie had turned up about a week ago. Mrs Hart had been working in the kitchen when she heard a noise from the cat flap. This had been quite a surprise as her cat had been run over the day before. She peered around the door and watched with amazement as a gently curved, black polished beak pushed a tiny posy of buttercups through the flap and dropped them onto the worn old coconut welcome mat in her hall. The face disappeared but emerged a few seconds later on the windowsill. The magpie poked four buttercups in through the outside opening of her kitchen ventilator unit. Satisfied with this opening gambit, the bird retired. Later that day Mrs Hart took her rubbish into the garden, and on the way to the bin was ambushed by the magpie who, yes that's right, pushed some buttercups into her slipper. You can guess the rest. Mrs Hart was treated to the full body decoration ritual, as was everyone who visited.

Standing in the back garden, listening to this unique tale, I packed away my cameras when Mrs Hart suddenly screamed 'Look out!' just at the moment that my right eardrum seemed to explode. The magpie had landed on my shoulder and enthusiastically rammed home yet more flowers, this time into my ear. It may be a fact little known to science, but I swear that a magpie beak is made of hardened tungsten. It is equipped with all the finesse and delicacy of a pneumatic road-drill. My inner ear felt as if it was being thoroughly explored by a diminutive coal miner. A second later I felt the slow, warm spread of blood trickling down my neck. But by then magpie had already disappeared.

'Crazy bloody bird' I cursed, clutching my wounded ear.

Just then Mrs Hart squeaked for a second time, 'Look out!'

Having worked out the modus operandi of this rampant magpie, I knew exactly where it would deposit the delicate yellow flowers clutched in its murderous beak. My left ear was the only unfilled cavity. I didn't need warning a second time. The garden was long and thin and I must have shattered the Shropshire sprint record on my way back to the house. Safe inside the kitchen, I stopped to watch the action outside through the impenetrable barrier of the kitchen window.

Mrs Hart strolled calmly along the garden path, seemingly impervious to the attentions of the demented magpie and its floral weaponry. She reached the house unscathed, while the bird aimlessly hopped around the lawn. This was a very focused animal: it had just one thing on its mind. The buttercups were intended for a specific target and there could be no substitute. Unfairly and suddenly deprived of its intended victim, the buttercups became superfluous and were discarded casually on the lawn. The disappointed magpie looked around the garden, as if to make certain that his prey had truly vanished. He then took to the air and departed.

Mrs Hart opened the kitchen door and said,

'Sorry. Should have warned you about that first. Maggie does it to everybody, but only once. After that you're safe. Got me in both ears. You were lucky.'

Just at that precise moment, lucky wasn't the adjective that immediately sprung to mind. The blood was congealing and blocking my ear. The right hand side of my world was already distant and muffled by a throbbing roar that took an hour to subside. For some inexplicably polite reason, I warmly thanked Mrs Hart for allowing me the opportunity of meeting Maggie and then left as rapidly as possible.

On the drive home I tried to work out a plausible explanation for this bizarre behaviour. What possible set of circumstances could have resulted in this unbelievable performance? And the truth is I couldn't even begin to guess. Wild magpies go to great lengths to avoid humans, but not this one. Maybe Maggie had escaped from a zoo; a hand-reared magpie can be incredibly tame. That would account for its lack of fear but does not even begin to explain the obsession for flower-stuffing. I was completely baffled.

Since then my mind has often drifted back to that strange day. I've come up with dozens of outlandish theories and discounted them immediately. Nothing in all my working experience with wild birds offers any clues to the origins of that incomprehensible conduct. In my office are boxes of photographs showing a magpie picking a string of buttercups and carrying them menacingly towards the camera. The bird looks wonderful, the pictures are technically fine and all of them are completely useless. No wildlife magazine or book, with the single exception of this one, will ever print them because, of course, magpies never – ever pick flowers. All of that pain was for nothing. But what really haunts me on dark sleepless nights or on casual strolls over weedy lawns, is the thought that the lunatic magpie is still out there somewhere. If there isn't an ancient Chinese proverb covering this risk to life and limb, then perhaps its time to fill the void. I'll invent my own:

'Beware of the magpie that picks buttercups.' Let this be a warning. If ever you see a magpie anywhere near a vaguely yellow flower – run like hell.

7

Rooks in Their Castles

Birds are, by and large, delicate and vulnerable creatures. On the surface their lives seem to be untroubled but they are enthusiastically chased and eaten by an impressive assortment of big, fast hunters. As humans it is probably impossible for us to imagine an existence in which potentially lethal danger might lurk behind every tree, every minute of every day. Living with this constant hazard, understandably, makes them wary of any large moving object that tries to get too close, which is why humans find it so difficult to get close enough to a wild bird to get a photograph.

In my job rooks pose the worst possible combination of problems. They are extremely bright, deeply suspicious and build their nests high in the treetops well away from prying eyes. Getting an inside view of their secretive family life is agonisingly slow and demands more than a little skulduggery. But on the few occasions I have taken the trouble to look into their lofty world, the rooks' inventive and curious minds make them fascinating beasts to watch.

One ice-cold February morning, when the bare bones of the forest branches were grey and free of leaf buds, I started making a scaffolding tower that ended up more than twice the height of a house. It was built in a small oak woodland on the edge of a Welsh farm. The ancient trees offered the perfect site for nesting rooks, and the birds had returned here to raise families every year for as long as anyone could remember. Scattered high amongst the tree tops were the solid silhouettes of last year's nests. A bit untidy and ragged after a long winter but, with just a bit of mending, they would be used again this spring. It was still winter when my building project began, and far too bleak for any rook to worry about nesting. At that time of the year they spend every waking hour just trying to find enough food to keep alive; nesting has to wait until the weather is less brutal.

But, because it would take many weeks to complete, the tower had to be started long before it was needed. I had to work without disturbing the birds, or the plan would be finished before it had even started. Every evening the rooks returned to the nesting grounds to sleep; they sometimes even came back during the day when the weather was particularly bad. They could safely doze in the treetops knowing that nothing could reach them. If any hungry enemy did try to creep near, more than three dozen pairs of eyes and ears provided a perfect early warning system. The rooks felt comfortable in this wood and to avoid alarming them I only worked for half an hour a day, around noon when they were out feeding. If the rooks had ever grown suspicious or agitated they might just have abandoned the copse and nested somewhere else.

Bolting the aluminium poles together was depressingly slow and progress was almost imperceptible. The pylon seemed to grow no faster than the sleeping trees around. The woodland belonged to Dilwyn Roberts; he was the sixth generation of his family to tend the farm. Dilwyn, just like the rooks, was an integral part of the landscape's history. Farming wasn't merely a job for him, he really loved the land and had a passionate interest in the animals that lived around him. He had a mixed farm of arable crops, sheep and a small herd of cattle. He was very fond of his rooks, an attitude that was highly unusual as most farmers loathe the very sight of these birds.

Dilwyn worked alone and never said very much; the longest sentence I ever heard him utter was about the rooks.

'They're comical beasts, strutting around the fields and sticking their noses in cow-pats.' This perfectly described the rooks' habit of searching fresh dung for flies and worms. They have long black legs, topped with shaggy feathers, and they seem to bounce around a field like agitated mechanical toys.

Conditions were bitterly cold for the first few weeks of building. There was frost every morning and the woodland plants waited for warmer weather before they would start to grow again. The meadows were carpeted with the listless pale green grass of winter, so every day Dilwyn would drive past on his noisy, spluttering antique tractor carrying bales of hay to the hungry sheep out in the far fields. One morning, while I was balanced precariously on top of the tower fitting a new piece of scaffolding, he stopped the tractor at the edge of the wood, climbed down and stomped over. He stared up intently for a few seconds then shouted up 'Bred any good rooks lately?' and then, hooting with agricultural glee, wandered back to his tractor.

I had no idea of building regulations and, without realising, broke every rule covering the construction of scaffolding. It was only afterwards that I discovered the tower was too high, it wasn't secured well enough, didn't contain enough bars, had no safety ladder and shouldn't have been built without help. That last point I had already managed to work out for myself. At first the job was simple but as the tower grew so did the difficulties. I just hadn't realised how hard it could be to climb up scaffolding while holding onto a pole twice my height and then try to bolt it on, while wobbling dangerously on a bar as thin as my wrist. The temperature may have been low but every day I left the wood dripping with sweat and vowing next time to work with moles.

Eight weeks later the tower was eventually finished. The aluminium skeleton was lashed to nearby trees with strong ropes and on the very top sat a platform of thick wooden planks that supported the small canvas tent where I would sit and watch the rooks. The scaffolding pipes, carefully painted dull green, melted into the thickening background of the forest canopy. The tower may have been high, but its components were slender; soon the odd looking creation was completely invisible, hidden in the light green growth of new spring leaves.

Birds have to choose carefully the time to begin nesting. If they start too early, there may not be enough food available for the chicks. If they leave it too late, the young birds won't have time to grow and master the techniques of survival before the onslaught of the next winter. When the rooks were eventually convinced that all traces of bad weather had vanished, they returned to breed in the site that had been used by their ancestors for at least a century. Maybe a hundred and fifty generations of

rooks had been hatched in these trees. Within a few days of their arrival the birds were worked up into a frenzy of preparation and, as always, they had timed their activity to perfection. Once last year's nests had been patched and repaired, and the birds had sorted out ownership rights, spring appeared in a gentle explosion of sunshine. Suddenly food became ridiculously easy to find, snacks came in the form of the countless worms and creepy-crawlies that emerged in the first warmth of the year. With full stomachs the rooks could then afford to turn most of their efforts to nesting. Early one morning, with Dilwyn to act as decoy, I clambered up the tower and for the next ten hours sat tucked away in the tiny canvas cubby-hole on top of the scaffolding; the rooks were completely unaware they were being watched and carried on their lives as normal.

The rookery was home to twenty-two nests, all built close together in just five trees. It was the bird equivalent of a multi-storey tower block, which is a surprising arrangement as rooks are argumentative birds that spend half their time rowing with neighbours. Woe betide any cavalier rook that misjudged his landing and wandered too close to another nest, or even infringed its airspace. The intruder would be greeted with righteous indignation followed by raucous screams and savage thrusts of a long, rapier sharp beak.

In the noisy world of a breeding colony, sticks are highly prized assets to the obsessively house-proud rooks. For nine months of the year, rooks presumably ignore any stick they meet in their daily lives but in the spring these humble objects take on the status of religious icons. A top-of-the-range stick is cherished and diligently protected against all-comers. A stick, you may think, is just a stick, but they have to be exactly right to be included in a nest. Too long and they are impossible to carry, too short and they can't be woven into the platform. Ancient sticks are too stiff and unyielding, thorny sticks are simply out of the question. Misshapen sticks are awkward and uncomfortable, but the right stick is a gem that is worth its weight in gold. I long ago discovered that birds can see qualities in a twig that completely elude human eyes. A premium branch becomes a coveted object of desire to be zealously guarded or pilfered, depending upon who owns it.

Rooks have a healthy piratical side to their nature, which is never more visible than in spring. I could clearly see the comings and goings of almost fifty birds and it was fascinating to watch how they interacted amongst themselves. Even once the eggs were laid, the nest owners were never completely satisfied with the architecture of their home. I always found this difficult to understand as rook nests are an untidy clump of tangled debris and no two nests are the same. But for no apparent reason, twigs that were perfectly acceptable last week were suddenly deemed to be unsatisfactory and disdainfully hurled out. Then new, presumably superior, twigs were brought in to replace them. Usually the new branches looked absolutely identical to the old ones that had just been thrown away.

I was about to leave the hide one evening when a rook came back to its nest, carrying a valuable addition to its nursery. The bird landed silently, threw back its head and cawed triumphantly while the two newly hatched

A tiny long-eared bat that brought a television studio to a standstill

Hen harrier

Millions of voles live on motorway verges, hidden and completely unnoticed

Fox in a meadow of cowslips: what you can't see are the chocolates

Crow searching for cunningly baited food on a motorway verge

Raven. One of the intellectual giants of the bird world

The magpie looked remarkably innocent until it launched its buttercup offensive

Rooks make conscientious, attentive parents

A young cuckoo with its wren foster-parent: a ridiculously unbalanced relationship

(Above) The pine marten is wild, the background is designer-built
(Right) Gibbons are the alarm clocks of the forest

Orphaned orang-utans often cling to each other for mutual comfort

It is impossible not to see a close relationship between orang-utans and humans

(Left) Wildlife photography is often a frustrating and bemusing task
(Below) Male orang-utan

An orang-utan prepares its attack on my canoe

chicks watched their mother perform her noisy celebration. For once I could see why she was so pleased for this truly was a prince amongst twigs. From God alone knows where, this bird had collected the battered remains of a squash racquet. The handle had disappeared and part of the head was missing. One or two of the strings still clung on, but this racquet hadn't seen a squash court in a very long time. However that was irrelevant – this may have been a piece of junk that was tossed onto a scrap heap but from that moment on it became the rook's most treasured possession.

The jubilant bird picked up the antique wooden crescent and delicately wedged one end into the heap of twigs. But, being an arc, as it was pushed further in, the far end would curve around and come out somewhere else. Having successfully pushed the racquet into the nest, the rook hopped over to the emerged end and poked that back, of course that then meant that the far side would again slide out. The persistent bird pushed and poked at least a dozen times as the unco-operative squash racquet see-sawed in and out of her nest. Try as she might the rook couldn't keep it in place. I could almost hear her snort with frustration. Eventually the racquet head was plucked out and laid flat on top of the nest. Content that redecoration was complete the bird took to the air and disappeared into the gloom of the treetops.

Within moments the rook from next door landed on the nest, picked up the racquet and whipped it back to her own place. The raid took just a few seconds and was a thoroughly professional job. The burglar then went through exactly the same process of fitting the strange piece of wood into place, only she took even longer deciding exactly where to place her booty to its best effect.

Needless to say when the rightful owner returned, she noticed the theft. At the first available opportunity she darted next door, grabbed the racquet, and carried it home. Over the next week that old lump of sports equipment travelled through the air literally dozens of times. I always expected the birds to come to blows over ownership, but they were very civilised about it. They were both careful to avoid direct challenges and only launched pillaging raids when the opposition was absent. Each time a rook landed in its rival's nest, the resident chicks responded by screaming for food. But this was war and the racquet robbers had just one thing on their mind, to grab the treasure and run. The chicks were totally ignored, much to their frustration.

The spring was near perfect; the sky seemed permanently blue and the sun shone endlessly. This was the weather of childhood memories and it was no real hardship to sit, unnoticed, in the treetops as all around the rooks carried on their busy lives. One of the great privileges of seeing into this secret world is getting to know individual youngsters and to watch how they develop and learn to cope with the rigours of life. The closest nest to the hide was almost within arm's reach. It was home to two chicks. I had missed the hatching of the elder bird but had been lucky enough to watch the second scramble from its egg after a two-hour fight to get free. Once the damp creature had dragged itself out, it was so weak that it collapsed face first onto the squash racquet. Within an hour it had dried out and was strong enough to scream for food when its mother returned to the nest. Baby birds need to learn quickly if they are going to survive.

Over just one month the two rook chicks grew from ugly, bald and helpless gargoyles into active, beautiful birds that were eager to explore the exciting world around. The chicks had hatched two days apart and, even with such a tiny difference in age, the older one was nearly twice as big as his sibling. From inside the hide I could see twenty-one chicks scattered in the trees around. By now the further nests were screened by thick banks of leaves. The chicks had all hatched in one fourteen-day period; they varied in scale from sparrow-size to dove-size, but they didn't all look the same. While every other young rook in the colony was sleek and well groomed, the two directly in front of me had obviously inherited some scruffy genes.

Their newly erupting feathers, instead of lying back neatly close to the skin, stood up in vague and untidy tufts, giving an appearance that owed much to a porcupine. Because they were the closest, I got to know these two chicks best of all and, purely privately, came to know them as Spiky Major and Spiky Minor. They were a joy to watch as each had their own distinct character. Spiky Major, being older, was a sophisticate experienced in the ways of the forest. Nothing disturbed or impressed him, apart from food. He was laid back to the point of near hibernation. Minor, on the other hand, was a hyperactive enthusiast. He spent almost every waking hour relentlessly exploring the nest – he was never still. Young rooks cannot honestly be described as either agile or nimble, so moving was a slow and clumsy process. At this stage the chicks' co-ordination is poor and they are still learning to control wayward and unco-operative limbs. Wherever Minor sat, after a few seconds he inevitably wanted to be somewhere else and would have to clamber over his big brother to get there. He would often jab his sharp claws onto Major's face to start the ascent. Having reached the pinnacle he would then sit on his brother's head to catch his breath before descending the long sloping back. On reaching the other side of the nest, Minor would scan the horizon for a few seconds and then turn around to make the return journey to where he started, only to retrace his journey immediately.

The endlessly patient and stoical Major was trampled every few minutes and never once retaliated. Several times a day Minor caught sight of his reflection in Major's bright piercing eye; he would study it for a second and then peck sharply. Rooks' beaks are formidable weapons; Major soon learned to close the eye nearest to Minor whenever he showed too much interest.

Spiky Minor was insatiably curious; the sound of a distant tractor or calling pheasant would immediately bring him to his feet. He would stand on the edge of the nest straining eagerly towards the source of the sound, trying to get closer and investigate. The arrival of a fly would send him into paroxysms of delight and curiosity. With arthritically slow movements, he crept across the nest, stalking the unsuspecting insect. The fly would almost always see him coming and disappear but occasionally Minor's efforts were rewarded and the insect didn't move. The scruffy young rook would sit and study the tiny creature, cocking his head slowly from left to right and back again. Like a stately old pendulum clock his head tipped from side to side until he could resist no longer and made an awkward lunge for the fly. He never once came close to catching one.

Young rooks stay in their nests for about four weeks. As the time approaches for them to leave, they become ever more active and spend most of their days stretching untried wings in preparation for the first flight. Exactly one month after Spiky Minor struggled out of his egg, I quietly climbed the scaffolding knowing that this could well be the last day I spent with the now familiar birds. It had been an early start and by six o'clock I was settled in my artificial eyrie sipping coffee from a flask and watching the forest come to life. Somewhere nearby a hidden wood warbler sang its complex territorial song to keep away rivals that might be planning to invade his patch of woodland. A great spotted woodpecker drummed dramatically on a huge ash tree not far away. It was still early but the soft sun was surprisingly warm. The adult rooks were already out hunting in the neighbouring fields while Major and Minor were both lying flat out on the nest, with their beaks open wide. Birds cannot sweat; they keep cool by panting like a dog and they needed to in this weather.

A handsome speckled wood butterfly landed in a pool of sunlight on the nest edge. Minor spotted the movement and began to move forward with reptilian slowness – and as he did so the forest all around us seemed to explode in a violent storm of noise and destruction. As I watched, Spiky Major disappeared in an ugly cloud of blood and feathers; poor Minor was less fortunate, his left wing was shredded and he hopped frantically around the nest platform, squealing with pain and fear before losing balance and toppling to the hidden ground below.

The peaceful morning was torn apart by twenty or thirty shotgun blasts ripping through the forest canopy. The few nests I could see simply disintegrated, along with their residents. From the ground, my camouflaged hide was completely concealed and the gunmen beneath had no way of knowing that there was a human sitting high up in the trees amongst the rooks. Fortunately the flimsy canvas hide was built onto thick oak planking that was impervious to shotgun pellets. I was terrified and curled up in a ball on the floor. In truth, there was probably no real danger but I had to lie and listen while all around, the birds I watched for so long were being blown to pieces. The appalling noise stopped as suddenly as it had started but I didn't want to move until the hunters had long gone. After finally getting up and looking out a few minutes later, I wished I hadn't. The rookery was annihilated. Corpses were festooned around the wood. Feathers and wings hung from the branches. Chicks, many younger than the Spiky brothers, died where they lay while some of the older birds had tried to leave in their panic. Most hadn't survived.

In some parts of the country this is an annual event. Rookeries are destroyed each spring to wipe out the new generation of rooks before they become a threat to growing crops. There is no doubt that rooks do cause problems for farmers because of their habit of eating newly sown seed.

Everyone is familiar with those tatty home-made manikins dressed in old clothes standing in the middle of fields. Today we call them scarecrows but in fact crows do little harm to crops; it is their cousins the rooks that are the real culprits. The name scarecrow was coined before species were well defined and each area had its own local words for animals. The terms rook and crow were sometimes interchangeable. Today bird names have been standardised and the guardians of the fields should be renamed scarerooks.

I don't have a farm and hordes of rampaging rooks do not eat into my profits. Farmers are in business and have every right to defend their interests but most do the task using less destructive methods. My friend Dilwyn had nothing to do with the shooting party; the killing had been carried out by a self-appointed band of hunters who were happy to wipe out rooks wherever they could found them. This rookery was easily accessible from the road, the men just parked their cars, spent two minutes doing the deed and drove off before anyone could react. They may have been local farmers who had suffered from rooks or simply hunters looking for an excuse to kill; I never did discover the identity of the culprits.

Not all of the youngsters died in the attack and the survivors, together with the adults who had been safely out hunting, returned the following year to build their nests in the traditional site. Twelve months later, almost to the day, those too were wiped out in an early morning raid. It's happened for decades and is probably still happening today. In an age when wildlife is being destroyed all around us, the gruesome slaughter of the rooks was very hard to take at close quarters. And, to be honest, I had come to see the Spiky brothers as friends. Watching them die was one of the most miserable experiences of my life.

8

Squatting with Troglodytes

Early one morning I had a telephone call from a friend who lived across the border in Wales. I had known Tim for more than twenty years; in the dim and distant past he had been my German teacher at school and, at that time, was a monstrously terrifying figure that haunted my nightmares. To a small twelve year-old, Mr Roberts appeared to be the size of a mature oak tree and an unfettered elemental force that brooked no challenge. Rancid Roberts, as he was known when well out of earshot, possessed all of the necessary weapons needed to keep control of any group of spotty adolescents. His hands were as big as shovels and over long years of teaching he had perfected a thunderous scowl that could melt cheese at two hundred paces.

I always imagined that he practised and honed his fearsome expression in front of the mirror in the privacy of his bathroom. But genes were on his side too; nature had equipped him with a voice that would be the envy of a healthy bull moose. When angry, a state that approximately co-incided with the hours of daylight, the man could be heard several towns away, making windows and children shake for acres around. Tuesday mornings and Thursday afternoons were truly the black spots of my existence. For what seemed to be several hours Mr Roberts pounded my aching and unwilling brain with incomprehensible words that contained an unnatural number of syllables. Images of huge German teachers caused me far more angst and sleepless nights than the onset of puberty. Rancid and I were totally incompatible and it was with mutual relief that we parted company after the unavoidable, disastrous exam at the end of the course.

Occasionally, afterwards, I saw him sweeping along the dusty school corridors like a malignant tsunami but by then my utter rejection of the German language meant that I was unworthy of even the mildest torture. When school finally ended, all memories of Rancid faded, or were at least relegated to the furthest recesses of my mind together with a desire to be the first man on the moon and an unreasonable love of pickled walnuts. I gave no thought to him for fifteen years until we accidentally met many years later at a conservation group meeting. I had just finished giving a talk on owls and was packing up my equipment when a perfectly ordinary man introduced himself with the words 'I bet you don't remember me'. And he was absolutely right. This man was no taller than the rest of the audience and only had one head. It was only when he stuck out his hand and said, 'Roberts, German teacher', that the awful sensations came flooding over me. How could this pleasant looking person possibly be the misanthropic ogre of my teenage nightmares? Catapulted back to the horrors of German declensions, I was too thunderstruck to make any sort of articulate reply.

Rancid made a few well-observed comments on my talk and asked questions that showed a real insight into the subject. Apparently he had been watching tawny owls in a nearby wood for decades. In the next few minutes one of the foundation bricks that made up the storehouse of my school memories suddenly crumbled to dust. It started to dawn on me that here was a kind and gentle man, a kindred soul who shared my interest in wild and empty landscapes. He then bought me a coffee and told tales of his long summer holidays away from school. Instead of boiling infants or laying waste entire villages as we unwilling German scholars liked to imagine, Mr Roberts had gone on wildlife expeditions to exciting parts of the world. At the very time I was only fantasising about such adventures, he was living them in the tropics and the Arctic.

It was only then that I realised just how unfair and comprehensively wrong a twelve year-old can be when viewing adults. With the wisdom of hindsight I could see that my erstwhile German teacher had an awesomely ferocious bark and absolutely no bite at all. I couldn't recall him ever doing anything to anyone, apart from shout. After two decades on the receiving end of my distorted judgement, Rancid Roberts had miraculously turned into a decent and interesting man who was truly worth knowing. His depth of knowledge was impressive and passionate. We kept in touch, on and off, over the years. When Tim eventually retired, he had plenty of time to explore the countryside he loved. The moment he asked me to call him 'Tim' is still one I cherish. The use of Rancid's first name at school would probably have resulted in capital punishment, and all these years later I still find it hard to say without feeling the need to look over my shoulder first.

That June morning Tim had just come back from walking his dog and telephoned to say that he had discovered a bird's nest – or at least what was left of one.

'I've found a cuckoo's nest.' He explained excitedly. 'Well no. I've found a cuckoo in a nest. A wren's nest can you believe.'

From almost anyone else I would have been very sceptical about this news. But Tim had been watching wildlife for a lot longer than I had and was not likely to make many mistakes. Even so, cuckoos are more than forty times the weight of a wren; it just didn't seem possible that the two species could ever get together in even the most one-sided relationship.

I was intrigued and arranged to meet him that afternoon to look at the nest. One week after retiring from thirty years of teaching Tim had bought Flossie, a huge shaggy English sheepdog, as an excuse to go walking every day. That morning they had explored a footpath in the Tanat valley: it was there that they found the nest and its unlikely occupant. The Welsh Marches are a labyrinth of narrow, unmarked lanes that are a frustrating maze to the uninitiated. It took me a while to find the small crossroads where Tim would be waiting. It's always been a mystery why walkers and holidaymakers so often overlook this part of Wales. They trundle through in their hundreds of thousands every year, *en route* to Snowdonia and the coast, driving through some of the prettiest scenery in the country without ever stopping. But at least this meant the roads were quiet and soon I found Tim leaning on a fence watching a pair of buzzards floating in the flawless blue sky. He came striding over and announced:

'The nest is just along this path. It's built into the roots of a huge old tree that must have fallen down years ago and, to tell the truth, Flossie found it. She was bounding ahead of me and suddenly began barking like a lunatic. And, well there it was. A baby cuckoo.'

Tim led the way along an overgrown path that left the main road at a right-angle; it was one of the old sheep farmers' hill-tracks that was in use long before the introduction of cars. The narrow path was tucked between two tall hedges whose lower branches had been cropped by cattle but the higher canopy spread like parasols and met across the gap to form a beautiful leafy tunnel that wandered gently uphill. After a ten-minute walk Tim stopped next to a panting and very excited Flossie who had reached the spot long before us. She was standing near an ancient and ramshackle wooden gate, the kind that can be seen almost everywhere in Wales and, judging from its state of repair, seemed to date back to at least the eleventh century. This one was held together with a Gordian knot of blue bailing twine and, if the number of frayed ends were anything to go by, the gate had been patched up more times than I could count.

The ailing gate once hung from a thick rough-sawn post which was now rotted through and would have completely collapsed if it hadn't been nailed to a massive fallen ash tree right next to it. I've always thought that overturned trees look terribly forlorn: ripped from the ground the exposed root systems remind me of skeletons and this was no exception. I could easily imagine the irresistible winter storms that first made this tree sway backwards and forwards, until one almighty gust pushed the trunk just a bit too far. The roots that once anchored the giant to the earth would have ripped out with a dreadful groan that marked the tree's death knell.

Years later the smaller roots had rotted or were still embedded in the ground, severed when the tree toppled. Only the thickest stems remained attached to the trunk, intertwined and sticking out in all directions. The grotesque suspended root system now formed a horizontal cliff-face that was at least twice my height. Above my head were iron-hard clumps of earth jammed into the few crevices that were sheltered from the rain; they were baked like clay and must have been there for the long years since the tree had died. It was a sad sight but for once I didn't dwell on the matter because just then Tim reached out a long bony finger and pointed, deep into the gloom of the tangled sticks, at a pair of bulging, gleaming black eyes. The young cuckoo was the same brown mottled colour as the hard earth packed around the roots; the camouflage was perfect. The bird crouched low on a dishevelled mattress of sheeps' wool, moss, feathers and hay that lay on one of the thickest roots.

Adult cuckoos are paranoically shy creatures that are almost impossible to watch at close range but youngsters are much more relaxed and are unruffled by anything. The bird sat blinking slowly, showing no interest in his visitors. Then Tim said 'There. Look. It hasn't moved at all.'

And, at the sound of his voice, the cuckoo lunged hysterically forward and started to squeal frantically. These truly are enormous birds with insatiable appetites and the adopted foster parents work far harder rearing a single cuckoo than they ever would bringing up an entire brood of chicks their own size. Young cuckoos take no chances with their food supply: to guarantee getting every scrap of available nutrition, they throw out any eggs or chicks belonging to the rightful owner. When a cuckoo hatches it is genetically programmed to push any other object out of the nest. Originally the adult wrens may have started off with ten eggs of their own but, when the intruder appeared, these would all have been ousted. Because wrens can't count, they would never have noticed that the size of their family had dramatically reduced, and would have carried on as normal. Only then, the cuckoo would receive all of the food.

A cuckoo stays in the nest for much longer than ordinary chicks and the increasingly weary adults have to bring in more than twice the normal amount of food to stoke its ravenous hunger. Young cuckoos are eating machines. They are permanently hungry and try desperately to increase their food intake by begging pitifully from any moving object within reach. It doesn't have to be their foster parents; it doesn't even have to be a bird.

We were close and the chick obviously thought that there was just a remote chance that we might be carrying worms or spiders so the optimistic young cuckoo tried his luck and begged. As we watched the chick's mouth gaped open, showing the cavernous bright red interior that is the mesmeric trigger that obliges parent birds to stuff food inside. The instinct to fill this mouth is so powerful that sometimes passing birds, that have nothing to do with the nest, will stop and give the cuckoo food that was originally destined for their own chicks. This is a very clever trick on the part of the cuckoo and it was now putting on a full-blooded performance for us. For over a minute the bird squawked and stretched, stridently demanding its feast; eventually it realised we weren't going to co-operate and suddenly stopped before giving a thorough shake and settling back down onto a branch to doze.

The scientific name for the wren is *troglodytes*, which means cave-dweller. Although the logic may be sometimes obscure, zoologists usually have some concrete reason for the names they give birds and *troglodytes* was chosen because of the wrens' distinctive domed-shaped nests. Imagine a ball, about the size of a clenched fist; in the front is a tiny entrance hole

Young cuckoo waiting for lunch

just large enough for the diminutive wrens to squeeze through. It really does look like a miniature cave. But this particular nest had long gone and the untidy remnants decorated the roots and undergrowth all around the cuckoo. The chick had grown so big that it had burst out of its former home and was now surrounded by the debris. The stranded youngster was still too young to fly so it simply sat impatiently and awaited the return of its adopted parents. The idea of a wren feeding a cuckoo was irresistible. I couldn't remember ever seeing this behaviour recorded on film before. We stayed for just a few minutes, knowing that the adult wrens would be somewhere nearby, ready to ferry more food to the waiting cuckoo.

Walking back along the path Tim said, 'Just how the hell do you suppose a cuckoo managed to lay an egg inside that nest?'

The same thought had been running through my mind. A fully-grown female cuckoo is about three times the size of a wren's nest – together with its occupants. But cuckoos are wonderfully skilled at their particular brand of piracy; females become specialists in finding the nests of just one type of bird and the choice is not their own. Cuckoos lay their eggs in the nests of the species that reared them when they were young. Females brought up by robins will lay their own eggs in robins' nests, those fed by reed warblers continue the family tradition by abandoning their unhatched offspring in the nest of a reed warbler. A female cuckoo lays about twelve eggs a year and each is left in a different nest, but always belonging to just one species.

The entrance to a wren's nest is low down, to keep out the worst of the wind and rain. The only way the female cuckoo could have put an egg inside would have been to sit on top and lay it by touch, through a hole that was slightly smaller than the egg itself. The mother of our baby cuckoo had to perform some interesting gymnastics twelve times that spring. I could almost imagine her gripping tightly on with tiny feet, while her back end groped for the nest entrance. I just couldn't work out how the cuckoo could have precisely located a hole built into a soft ball, using a body that was covered in feathers. It seemed an impossible task. The mind boggled; it must have been like threading a needle in the dark, while wearing boxing gloves. With that surreal image still in my mind, an hour later I put up a small canvas hide on the far side of the track and the wrens were totally unconcerned by this arrival. From the shelter of an oak tree in the next field, I watched through binoculars as the wrens immediately came back to the nest without giving the hide a second glance. Over the next three days the hide was moved slowly closer to the upturned tree, until it was in the final position just two strides away from the nest. I had photographed cuckoos before, but not enough of them and never one being fed by a wren. This job would be fun.

Early one Tuesday morning, it was a weekday to reduce the chance of being disturbed by weekend walkers, I carried my heavy camera equipment along the path and from somewhere higher up the valley came a loud *cuck-koo*, the clear and unmistakable advert of a male searching for a mate. The female has a very different call which sounds like water being poured from a bottle. Hers is a musical bubbling cry nothing at all like the male's and is usually not recognised as belonging to a cuckoo. I had arranged to meet Tim there, as he would see me into the hide.

Before reaching the nest, I spotted shattered bits of timber scattered around the lane and it didn't take a mastermind to discover the source. Yesterday the field next to the path had been stocked with bullocks, young male cattle full of undirected energy. These, along with generations of their ancestors, must have spent thousands of hours rubbing themselves contentedly against the elderly gate until the decaying struts had finally given way and collapsed during the night. It was bound to happen sometime. But why did it have to be that particular night? Dozens of cloven-hoof prints in the soft earth showed that the bullocks had left the field to take advantage of their new-found freedom. In the process they had trampled the fallen gate and reduced it to splinters. Unfortunately the bullocks' vandalism hadn't stopped with the gate; my hide had completely disappeared. Guy ropes and tent pegs were strewn around the ground but the canvas itself had just vanished.

My hides are home-made from odds and ends that most people would throw away; the missing one was financially worthless but its loss had cost me a potentially fascinating opportunity. I looked around to try to salvage the situation and soon spotted, grazing in the centre of the field, a Friesian bullock sporting a green and brown camouflaged hide elegantly around his head and neck. The canvas swayed and flapped like an overgrown scarf. The animal must have been wearing the strange apparel for quite a while because it was totally unconcerned by its presence. As bullocks can be brought to the edge of panic stricken hysteria if a small paper bag blows too quickly across their field, this chap had obviously grown to accept the new addition to his appearance.

Walking slowly and quietly towards the steadily munching animal, I tried to reclaim my property but the bullock wouldn't let me anywhere near. As soon as I got within striking distance he galloped off clumsily, kicking his back legs wildly and tossing his head in the air. The other bullocks caught on immediately, they thought this was a wonderful new game and all joined in enthusiastically – on his side. Soon I was trying to winkle out a single animal from a careering herd of unruly adolescent cattle equipped with far more energy than brains. Sheepdogs might find it easy but I didn't. It wasn't hard to spot my bullock, as he was the only one wearing an oversized cravat, but the more I attempted to catch him, the more excited and frisky he became. For twenty minutes we raced around the field, with the bullock gang outrunning me easily. Until that moment I had never suspected that cattle have a sadistic streak to their nature. At the beginning of the game the bullocks would race from one end of the field to the other whenever I made a move. But as I grew increasingly tired, they would stop just out of my reach. If I took just one step, they would run forward a few paces, keeping far enough away to avoid me but close enough to tease.

In the end the animal was caught by its own lack of imagination. I managed to trap him in a corner of the field where he performed an elegant three-point turn in an attempt to escape. Unfortunately in the process he trod on one end of the trailing hide and this stopped him dead in his tracks. The canvas was wrapped around his neck at least twice and while his head was bent low, almost touching the ground, he stepped on the trailing end. This was tough, waterproof canvas that wouldn't be easily ripped. The bullock's head was pulled down while he fought valiantly to wrench it free, but he stubbornly refused to do the one thing that would have released him. He obviously just never thought of raising his foot and with his head forced low he couldn't see to run. He was trapped. With a last ditch effort, I leapt forward and caught his neck with one arm while trying to untangle the canvas with the other. Just at that moment the sound of voices floated across the grass.

'Just look at that. D'you think it's some kind of ancient Welsh tradition?'

'Cow wrestling is the only hobby people have round here. There's sod all else to do.'

The unmistakable flat Liverpool accents came from two teenagers peering over the hedge. While I struggled to hold the bullock, they looked on with mild interest.

'Could you give me a hand, please?' I yelled. 'This is caught around his head I can't shift it.'

'I'm not going in there, with that bull,' said one, 'just look at the size of its … er … paws. And it's got horns.'

'Look I'll hold it, you just pull the canvas off.' I explained imploringly.

'No chance,' came the reply.

Although they weren't keen to help, they were only too delighted to stand and watch as I slowly unravelled the hide from the bullock's neck. They helpfully provided a running commentary just in case I missed any of the salient points.

'I don't think this is an ordinary man. Ordinary men don't fight bulls. This is probably an Olympic event in Wales and he's practising for a big match coming up.'

'Well 'e won't **** well win then. The bull's still up and kicking but 'e looks completely knackered. Here now look, the bull's standing on his foot. I bet that hurts.'

It did. Bullocks are heavy and all of their weight rests on ridiculously small feet. Being stamped on is a bone-crunchingly painful experience.

'Shall we give 'im a hand?'

'Nah, that's his job. We're just tourists enjoying the sights.'

When the hide finally loosed its limpet-like hold on the bullock, I hobbled back to the lane, sweating like a pig and nursing several crushed toes. My unappreciative audience followed slowly.

'Did you know that your gate is broke?' said one of the lads.

'It's not my gate,' I panted 'I am not a farmer, I am here filming wildlife.'

I long ago learned that the word 'filming' carries a lot more clout than 'photographing' and I badly wanted to score points off these two. But, unimpressed, they just stood and watched as I took out a fresh hide from my rucksack.

'Going camping now are you?'

''E's not going to be very comfortable in that thing. 'E'll have to sleep standing up.'

'Don't you two have somewhere else to go?' I suggested helpfully and collapsed onto the grassy bank to examine the damage done to my feet. Faced with the fact that the interesting action was over, they wandered off down the track still moaning.

'That's probably the most interesting thing that's happened around 'ere for years,' said one voice. I couldn't hear the reply but no doubt it was along the same sarcastic lines.

Wrens are confiding little birds and the adults accepted the presence of my replacement hide without seeming to notice. Two days later I crept inside and sat down to wait for the birds to appear. Within five minutes a wren returned carrying a bouquet of still-wriggling caterpillars. The tiny adult landed on one of the thin guy ropes that held up my hide; it was close enough to touch. Through a viewing panel, the size of a garden pea, I could even see the row of tiny feathers around its eyes, feathers so delicate they look like eyelashes. The bird sat for a few seconds, flicking its stumpy tail and searching the surrounding landscape for any potential enemies that may be lurking nearby. The chick saw the movement and began to squawk and scream. By now the young cuckoo was simply vast, and it was absurd to see this colossus anxiously begging food from a bird that was scarcely bigger than my thumb. As if responding to an imperious command the wren flittered towards the remains of its nest. There were no twigs where the adult could perch so, looking exactly like a helicopter returning to an aircraft carrier, the wren simply landed on the chick's broad back. The cuckoo swivelled its neck, opened its beak and the wren's head and shoulders disappeared inside the mouth to drop the meal down into the voracious black hole in the centre.

Suddenly the wren stiffened and looked up. Out of the soft distant blanket of muffled farm sounds, two distinct voices began to emerge and grow closer. The wren slipped off quietly through the hedge and, with a sinking heart, I recognised the Merseyside twang of the lads that had plagued me forty-eight hours earlier. Of all the foul luck. They weren't day trippers, they must have been on a residential course studying geography or biology or some other cursed subject that a vindictive fate had decreed should be contemplated in this particular remote part of Wales. I felt unfairly persecuted; they weren't here to enjoy themselves, they should have been suffering like I did on my field trips. At that time of the day they should have been up to their calves in an ice-cold sticky bog examining spirogyra or half way up a wind-blown mountain mapping the finer points of a terminal moraine, but the academic charisma of a school field trip was obviously lost on them. So instead they wandered the hidden green lanes while their mates were observing the geological remnants of the last ice-age.

'D'you think that photographer prat will be here again?' said a disembodied voice.

'Who cares?' came the reply. I obviously had lost my appeal as a figure of entertainment and wasn't at all sure whether to be relieved or insulted by this lack of interest.

'Where was that tent thing of his?' came the first voice again.

'Dunno – all these trees look the same to me.'

'This Llanbuggery place is a hell of a long way to come for a party.'

'Yeah – but it was a good one all the same. Same again tonight?'

Suddenly I remembered that not every moment of field trips was unmitigated hell. After all they were residential trips, miles away from home and the scrutinous gaze of parents.

From where they stood the hide was hidden behind a bank of bramble and, for added camouflage, had been covered with leafy twigs and fronds of bracken. It was virtually invisible from the path. Through the tiny hole I could see the boys leaning against the huge fence post which had survived the bullock attack. They were lazily throwing stones into the nearby field. The grazing cows looked up for a second, but they are incredibly incurious beasts and soon went back to their ceaseless munching. One of the lads looked around, pulled down his zip and relieved himself noisily against the wooden post. Just at that moment a cow hidden on the far side of the hedge did what all herbivores do with monotonous regularity, it broke wind. This was not a polite, smothered, dining room fart; this was an unembarrassed, red-blooded, sheet-ripping explosion. Even by normally impressive cow standards it was a truly heroic effort. In the quiet of a secluded Welsh valley, the noise was spectacular and, unless you knew what it was, very alarming. With a startled lurch the unsuspecting boy staggered around looking for the source of the disturbance.

'What the **** …… Unnngggghaaahhhhhh!!!'

I didn't at all blame the lad for being caught short; it happens to everyone, and when the feeling strikes there is absolutely nothing wrong with nipping behind a hedge. But I really think he should have known better than to pee onto a live electric fence. Anyone with even a passing acquaintance of the countryside should have recognised the sharp metronomic clicking of a fence generator. After the gate had been smashed, the farmer had put up an electric fence to stop the cattle straying out of the field until he had time to put up a new gate.

Electric fences run off small batteries and, to save energy, they don't give out a constant charge. Electricity passes through in pulses, and each one is signalled by a sharp click. For the first time I felt a passing wave of sympathy: this lad had probably spend most of his life in a city and had maybe never been in a field before. This fleeting compassion soon passed when I noticed a very agitated wren sitting, with a beakful of spiders, on a rock at the edge of the path. If I moved or spoke now, the bird would notice and would lose its trust in the hide. I had been on the receiving end of fence shocks more than once and knew that the experience wasn't terminal, so I sat back quietly and watched the story unfold.

One of the many remarkable properties of water is that it is a wonderful conductor of electricity. The Liverpool lad must have had a large liquid content to his breakfast for he was in no hurry to finish. When the next inevitable click came, a pulse of high voltage electricity passed along the wire and up the stream of liquid. The water gave a far better contact than if he had touched the wire with his bare hand. The results were not disappointing.

'Arrrgggghhhhhhhh!!!' The spectacular scream really caught the attention of the cows; here was something entirely new which deserved a glance of four or even five seconds.

Shocks from electric fences are not as sharply painful as a thump on the nose or hammer on the thumbnail. It is more like a stunning blow to the whole system. Try and imagine what it would be like to be hit by a wet duvet travelling at thirty miles an hour. No single part of your body is particularly hurt but instead you feel as if you've been had been trampled by a herd of bison wearing slippers. The overall effect is temporary paralysis and this lad was completely stunned. Instead of moving away he just stood there, dribbling and moaning for another few seconds. When the third click brought another surge he bellowed with even more discomfort.

The other lad was much quicker on the uptake and showed a commendable concern for his friend's welfare. He yelled, 'Move yer stupid git'.

But his advice was unnecessary. The cumulative effect of the three shocks had tightened up his bladder muscles and the danger passed. By now his friend was reduced to a helpless heap; he leant quivering against the old gatepost sobbing with laughter. Tears poured down his cheeks and his chest heaved with the effort of trying to catch his breath. The amusement was strictly one-sided. With the fatally wounded dignity of a teenager whose carefully cultivated cool exterior has been shattered beyond retrieval, the poor lad just couldn't take any more and his shell of indifference cracked wide open.

With a yodel-like cry he shrieked 'I hate this ∗∗∗∗ place. I really hate it.'

He then stomped off down the path, leaving his friend to recover and finally follow. In less than a minute the wren came back to the nest to feed the ever-starving cuckoo chick. I stayed with the family of wrens for about ten hours in all, and would have completely forgotten the unfortunate lad if it weren't for the rhythmical click-click-click that dominated the noises filtering into the hide. Even now I can't hear the sound of an electric fence without feeling just a little pang of commiseration for the overworked wrens and the Liverpool schoolboys who never had the chance to see them.

9

Things That Go Burp
in the Night

The huge male orang-utan sat in the durian tree and stared down with an inscrutable face that was completely impossible to read. Unlike chimpanzees and gorillas, their close relatives, orang-utan faces do not give many clues to their state of mind. They always wear the same calm, vaguely melancholic expression while underneath, in their bright and creative brains, almost anything can be going on.

It had taken almost four days to find this animal. Orang-utans once lived all over south-east Asia but now, due to terrible overhunting and destruction of forest, they live only on the islands of Borneo and Sumatra. The word orang-utan is a Malay term that translates as 'man of the forest'. *Orang* means 'man' and *utan* is 'forest', which is why the name should never be shortened simply to orangs: this is seen as a terrible breach of etiquette.

According to local folklore orang-utans are the direct descendants of humans that long ago decided to live in the forest rather than in villages. I have no problem with this theory because, despite a thick covering of untidy bright orange hair, orang-utans have always seemed remarkably human to me. But that probably has more to do with their behaviour than their appearance. Chimpanzees are unpredictably mercurial: they can leap from whimsical playfulness to murderous rage in the blink of an eye. An angry male chimp is a potentially very dangerous animal; its teeth, hands and feet are all used as terrifyingly efficient weapons powered by bulging muscles that no human could hope to match. Few people ever feel totally relaxed in the company of wild chimps.

Their cousins, the gorillas, simply exude power. Although they are much bigger and stronger than chimpanzees, gorillas just don't feel as threatening. They rarely use their awesome strength aggressively but even when just sitting around, silverback males have a brooding presence that I've never sensed in any other animal and this is enough to unnerve even the toughest traveller.

Orang-utans on the other hand give the impression of being easygoing and completely relaxed. They are so laid-back that they seem to be permanently in a tranquil haze brought about by the chain smoking of highly illegal cigarettes. Orang-utans spend almost all of their lives in first gear; they are geologically slow and never seem to get worked up over anything. Through a narrow gap in the branches I could see the male above me lean forward and pluck a ripe durian; with banana-thick fingers he split open the skin and sucked out the juicy centre. Orang-utans absolutely adore durian fruit and will travel for days through the forest to reach a tree in fruit.

They have an amazingly geographical memory that we can't really fully appreciate. Each ape has a territory covering up to four hundred square miles of forest. To the inexperienced human eye, one bit of rain forest looks exactly like every other. The undergrowth can be so thick that it is impossible to see more than a few metres in any direction and the only landmarks are trees – millions and millions of trees that all look remarkably similar. It is like trying to negotiate a huge maze, where there are no corners or dead ends to use as guides. Yet somehow the orang-utan mentally stores the precise position of his favourite food trees; but what is truly incredible is that he also remembers exactly when they come into fruit. Central Borneo doesn't have set fruiting seasons like Britain; each tree has its own cycle that is different to the rest. The ape knows where to find the durian trees in his patch of forest and can also predict when their fruit will be ripe. A week before the fruit is at its best, the orang-utan will make a beeline for a good tree that may be three miles away, with a sense of timing and navigation that almost defies belief.

Although eating durians would probably be one of the greatest pleasures of his life, for all the excitement he showed this orang-utan might as well have been reading a telephone directory. Under similar circumstances in

Africa a chimpanzee would softly hoot with pleasure, while a gorilla would give out long low belches of contentment. But orang-utans have taken nonchalance to the level of an artform; they could almost have invented the concept of super-cool. The big male slowly munched his way through durian after durian; the pace of eating never altered and he didn't even seem to stop for a breath. With great long arms the animal could sit in one spot and harvest the crop from most of the nearby branches; once they were stripped he would move to a different branch and start all over again.

Orang-utans are the largest tree-dwelling animals on earth. Although they can walk easily on the ground, they usually choose not to bother. There is nothing to attract an orang-utan down onto the forest floor. The branches at tree-top level are interlocked to create a lush canopy of leaves that act as a giant parasol to shade everything beneath, making the ground so very dark that little can grow. Out of the thick layer of dead leaves, twigs, mosses and lichens that carpet the earth, there springs the occasional stunted plant, together with the thin stems of climbers that creep up the trunks of the nearest giant tree towards the light. While in the dense mass of the forest roof towering above, nearer the life-giving sun, there is an almost incomprehensible diversity of fruit, nuts, fresh leaves and flowers. In two square miles of Bornean rainforest there can be more species of trees than in the whole of Western Europe. Finding food is simple for orang-utans, as long as they stay high up where the growth is at its richest. This, inevitably, means that they are very difficult to photograph; having found this male all I could do was sit patiently until he came down to a branch that was low enough to see clearly. The orang-utan had been sitting in the tree for two days; I could only wait for him to move somewhere more accessible.

Orang-utans are horribly endangered. The world population is only around 24,000 animals and they all live in an environment that is steadily being wiped out by humans. The Indonesian rainforest, like that found everywhere else on the planet, is being cut down even now. As you read this page an area the size of three football pitches has been stripped of trees. Forest animals are specialists; they have evolved to live in just one place and when that disappears – so do they. Destruction of their habitat is just as lethal as a bullet through the brain.

Forests in Borneo aren't like those we know in Britain. They are dark, brooding and awkward to navigate. There are no roads and very few trails. This makes travelling physically hard work. Viciously thorned creepers snag clothes and dense patches of undergrowth often bar the route. While we are forced to keep at ground level, orang-utans move easily and confidently through their three-dimensional habitat. Slowly passing from tree to tree, they give absolutely no thought to innocent wildlife photographers waiting hopefully below. Should you ever see an orang-utan in a zoo, you would probably assume it would be difficult to lose such an extraordinary looking creature. They are huge, very hairy and come in a distinctive orange colour. Set against a bank of dark green leaves, they should – theoretically – be visible for miles around. Yet these apes have a mystical, ephemeral quality. In the thick shroud of leaves, high up in the dappled sunlight, orang-utans simply melt into the background and disappear from view. They sit quietly enveloped in the treetops, with a camouflage that would make a chameleon envious. To put it another way, orang-utans are real pigs to track down.

Reaching the elusive orang-utans was quite a chore. My destination was a huge tract of primary forest in central Kalimantan in southern Borneo. The fastest way of getting there was on water. In a rainforest, speed is strictly a relative measurement. I use the word 'fastest' in the sense that boats are marginally quicker than walking, but we are not talking about burning rubber. It had been a typically mundane start to the trip, beginning with a huge international airliner, progressing to a series of ever-smaller planes to finally reach a bumpy airstrip not far from the forest edge. It was then just a taxi ride to the nearby town to hire a boat.

The quays in these riverside villages are usually overflowing with boats of all shapes and sizes. Most belong to people from out in the surrounding forest who have come in for supplies; they arrive in canoes hollowed out with hand-axes from huge tree-trunks. This may be a trip made just three times a year and on the return leg the tiny vessel is so overloaded with sacks and boxes that the sides are barely visible above the waterline. But these are expert boatmen and with effortless ease they paddle upstream and disappear into the forest gloom with a cargo that would have Health and Safety Executive Inspectors apoplectic with shock back home in Britain.

The remaining boats around the quay are commercial craft that earn their living on the river wherever they can, through an unpredictable combination of fishing, transporting goods and acting as water-taxis. I needed to find a boat that would take me upstream deep into the forest and the problem was choosing the right one. It had to be someone who could be trusted to wait while I searched for the apes, who wouldn't get fed up and go home without me. I have friends who can spend a weekend in a new country and come back speaking like natives. They have a natural skill for languages that is completely missing in my genetic blueprint. I can always pick up a few essential phrases and sentences but never have enough time to learn more. Because my linguistic talents are woefully inadequate, I take the coward's way out and try to find a guide who can speak English. This totally unreasonable condition immediately rules out most contenders and, on this particular occasion, the remaining few had to be judged by the state of their boats.

Moored on the quay was an armada of craft in every possible state of repair. At the top end of the market were a couple of antique speedboats. Equipped with vast engines that were just too big for the boats, these belonged to the local boy racers – a species that can be found everywhere in the world. Anyone visiting a forest to see wildlife should avoid these monsters like the plague. The hideous noise made by a roaring speedboat will drive away any living animal within a radius of two miles. You may reach your destination a lot quicker but the local wildlife will be long gone before you get there. The huge wake created by a powerboat will erode the riverbank and maybe even swamp the nests of the hundreds of birds that live in the rich border zone between forest and river. I wanted something a lot slower and far less intrusive.

Even here in the open, where there was a slight breeze wafting over the water, the temperature was oppressive. Inside the forest, where no wind could penetrate, it would be stifling. Sweat trickled down my back and pools of water had already formed around my toes. My boots, and the feet inside, would not be dry again until I got back home. In conditions like this it is essential to drink little and often. After idly wandering along the waterfront for a few minutes I stopped for a quick sip of water from a plastic bottle in my camera bag. Then a quiet voice from behind asked,

'Would you like a cup of coffee?'

Tied to a half-rotten tree trunk nailed to the jetty was an ancient khlotok, the traditional, ubiquitous wooden long boats that work the waterways of Borneo. Sitting on its flat-roof was an Indonesian man, about my own age, dressed in impossibly ancient jeans and a brand-new Michael Jackson T-shirt. Indonesians are a polite and naturally friendly people. They start conversations with travellers, simply because they are interested in hearing their story. Strangers in these remote villages are few and far between, and are particularly welcomed. The locals have a simple marketing technique: they just sit and chat. They want to know everything about visitors, their families, homes and jobs. They are genuinely keen to learn and there is never a hint of a hard-sell. The man on the boat was boiling water in an old tin can, which looked as if it had started life as a catering pack of baked beans. The water was bubbling on an open fire built on top of the khlotok's wooden roof. This seemingly reckless approach to cooking and boat maintenance was more than enough to put me off any prospective captain, until I noticed the thick sheet of metal under the fire's glowing embers. The man stood and introduced himself; 'Hello, my name is Joaquin. Please come on.'

He gave me a cup of coffee but drank only water himself. The coffee was obviously a cunning ploy to lure in western travellers, but that only made him seem a more imaginative entrepreneur. At this stage there was no mention of hiring his boat; Joaquin sat and explained that he had been born in Borneo but went to the bright lights of Java when he was sixteen. For nine years he worked in a hotel in Jakarta, starting as a porter and working his way up to head of the mail office. He had studied English at night school and was obviously another of those blessed individuals who effortlessly absorb languages. His English was virtually flawless. 'My father died on my twenty-fifth birthday,' he explained. 'He left me all his belongings and this boat. So I came home.' The boat was now Joaquin's home and income. He was a charming, friendly character and I didn't have to look any further to find my boat. In Borneo there are no set rates for most services: the seller asks as much as he feels he can get and the buyer tries to knock down the asking price by at least fifty percent. Haggling is a way of life. But unlike in so many other countries, bargaining in Indonesia rarely gets hot-blooded; our negotiations were relaxed and over in minutes. Having gone through the obligatory routine of arguing over a fair price, honour was satisfied on both sides so Joaquin untied the boat and we went to pick food supplies from the local waterfront shop. An hour after I arrived we set off upstream towards the orang-utan forest.

Pure luck had dropped into my lap the best possible guide I could ever have found. Wildlife wasn't a problem; I had spent weeks researching facts about orang-utans and the animals that shared their forest. Packed in my bags was a small library of reference books that could give every detail about breeding, habitat and food. There wasn't a bird on the river that couldn't be identified within minutes. Joaquin had just a passing understanding of the local wildlife but he seemed to know everything else about the forest and its human culture.

As we chugged along the river, at around four miles an hour, he explained about the way the villages worked. He gave names to the few people we saw on the bank or bobbing along in ramshackle boats on the water. But, most fascinating of all, he pointed out plants that were used by the locals for an astonishing variety of unlikely jobs. He showed me plants that dyed cotton, plants that purged intestinal worms, plants that were used to marinade meat. This was an aspect of life in Borneo I would never have considered without Joaquin's expert help.

At first we passed villages and small settlements every mile or so but as the boat ventured deeper into the forest signs of human activity became increasingly scarce. The forest became thicker and more impressive; this was what I'd come to see. After eight hours we came across a single wooden house on the riverbank; in front was a tiny jetty on which there sat a teenage boy fishing. He wasn't using a rod, just a length of string and a hook, which he threw as far as possible across the river and dragged slowly back again through the black water. The wind was blowing downstream, carrying the dull coughing sound of the khlotok's diesel engine away from the jetty. It was a while before the fisherman noticed the boat, but once he had the boy quickly folded the line and dropped it into his pocket. He then stood up, stuck out his thumb and tried to hitch a lift. This was one of the glorious highpoints of my trip. I've seen hundreds of hopeful hitch-hikers on the Shrewsbury by-pass but never, ever, have I seen one trying his luck on a riverbank in a tropical rainforest. And, with no cars or roads for maybe eight hundred square miles, where had he learned the right hand signal? (I later discovered that he picked it up by watching re-runs of the old American TV series *The Dukes of Hazard*, while on his one and only trip to Jakarta a few months earlier.) Joaquin was at the back of the boat, casually holding the tiller with one hand. He turned to ask 'Is it fine if we pick up this man?' How could I possibly say no? We were probably the only boat that would pass by that day; in fact the next might not appear for another week.

Joaquin steered towards the tiny jetty and skilfully timed the mooring so that the boat bumped gently against the wooden supports and stopped dead. The boy jumped on board and Joaquin spoke to him in a language I couldn't follow. The meeting was less than cordial; the boy was obviously uncomfortable as Joaquin greeted him with, what seemed to be, a severe telling off. I couldn't understand a word of the monologue but the underlying message was unmistakable. Joaquin was very annoyed and, having made this crystal clear, returned to the tiller and the boat started steadily moving upstream again. The mysterious hitch-hiker climbed onto the flat roof, sat down and closed his eyes. Joaquin called to me:

'Miker.'

For some reason he always added a soft 'r' to the end of my name. He didn't do it with any other English word and I never did discover why it was only with this one.

'Miker. This is my nephew Wamena; he should be collecting fish but he wants to work on the boats. Do you mind if he comes with us?' The boat could easily sleep six people so, as far as I was concerned, Wamena was welcome to stay. We kept moving until about six o'clock when it became just too dark to see. Joaquin found a huge tree lying on the riverbank, where we would moor and spend the night. As soon as the engine was switched off Joaquin jumped onto the bank and tied a rope to the thick trunk, while Wamena dug the fishing line from his pocket and disappeared to the end of the boat. Joaquin then produced a huge flat sheet of blackened steel from the engine compartment, laid it on top of the boat roof and started to make a fire. Within five minutes Wamena was back, clutching two impressive fish. This time Joaquin spoke to him in English: 'Good job too, now prepare them.'

Wamena plucked a penknife from his voluminous trousers, slit open the underside of each fish and, with a finger, scooped out the insides and dropped them noisily into the water. We ate well that night, dining on fresh fish and rice, followed by bananas. Over the meal Wamena explained that Joaquin was teaching him English, but he was not a good student and didn't practise enough. As I couldn't have said such a complex sentence in Indonesian, it seemed that Joaquin was a skilled tutor and Wamena was keen to learn. Not for the first time did I humbly realise that English-speakers are often reprehensibly lazy. We can almost always find someone, anywhere in the world, who can speak our language and we have come to rely on it. Yet, here in a remote corner of a Borneo rainforest was a young boy who had already mastered the basics of a second language, without the advantages of an advanced educational system.

We were on the boat for another two days before reaching the stretch of forest where I hoped to track down the orang-utans. Joaquin was in charge of the boat, Wamena supplied the fish and I was free to watch the wildlife. It was hardly a taxing trip but now the real work had to begin. I already knew that the orang-utans would be very elusive and, until the apes had been found, it seemed a sensible precaution to hang onto the boat so that we could move to a different area if this first stop proved to be useless. The khlotok would be both home and transport for the next few weeks.

An hour after dawn on the first day in the search area, Joaquin and Wamena stayed on the boat while I ventured into the forest looking for the red apes. This was one of the most frustrating projects of my entire life; other travellers and researchers had reported that orang-utans lived nearby but could I find them? I have no wish to bore anyone with a diary of tedious hours spent searching the tree tops until my neck ached with the effort of constantly looking up – only to find nothing but a vast sea of leaves. This is the dull, uninspiring part of wildlife photography that tends to be overlooked, so I'll gloss over it by simply saying that my first search was a complete flop. Tired and disconsolate I got back to the boat, at the end of the second day, having spent a total of twenty-two hours in the forest without seeing so much as a discarded orang-utan hair. Joaquin was on the riverbank, fishing; he told me that Wamena had gone home. Apparently he was bored and had hitched a ride on a boat heading back downstream; this boy had a real talent for cadging lifts, a skill that I was forced to learn later in the trip.

It took more than three days to track down an orang-utan and it was noise that led me to it. After spending a fruitless morning in the forest I was about to walk back to the boat when the sound of tearing wood floated down from the canopy, this was immediately followed by a far more substantial object – a huge branch that landed at my feet. Peering up into the dense patchwork ceiling of miscellaneous greens, I spotted a movement that slowly turned into an arm. A huge, powerful arm that was at least three times the diameter of my own. This awesome limb was sparsely coated with long rust-red hair. I had found my first orang-utan.

The next few days were fascinating for me but would sound deadly dull on paper. I literally lived with the orang-utan, following slowly as he went from tree to tree, in search of food. Occasionally the huge male would drop down to the floor for no obvious reason and it was only then that I realised just how vast these creatures truly are. The first time he clambered down, my breath quite literally stopped. Male orang-utans are not big, they are colossal. They make Sumo wrestlers seem anorexic. They bulge and ripple in places where no animal has any right to have muscles in the first place. It is usually only the males that come down to the ground, for the simple reason that they are too big to have enemies. Even a Sumatran tiger would back off from one of these ape-mountains. Although it was uncomfortably intimidating to see such a massive animal at close quarters, at least it gave me the chance to really look at an orang-utan in detail. High in the treetops they were usually just shaggy silhouettes but on the ground they suddenly became flesh-and-blood.

Although apes are closely related to humans, there are some important differences and one of the most obvious is the way we each walk. While humans move around on two legs, apes are quadropedal – they walk on all fours. Orang-utans, like all of this family, can stand on their hind legs only for a short time, but they are not comfortable and soon drop back on all fours. Their back legs end in feet that are much like our own. But their front legs are equipped with hands that must be able both to manipulate objects and be used for walking. To achieve this seemingly contradictory combination apes don't walk on their palms, as most people seem to think; they walk on knuckles or clenched fists. This keeps the sensitive fingers tips curled up away from the ground, stopping them becoming too callused and unusable.

My first male orang-utan spent three days in a tree before venturing down to the forest floor. Orang-utans are excellent at climbing, but they are slow and methodical. They never take chances and carefully check the load-bearing qualities of a branch before trusting it with their full weight. Some break under the strain, which explains the falling branch that nearly finished my trip before it ever really got started. It took a long time for the orang-utan to reach the ground and only when he sat at the base of his tree did I notice that he was carrying a durian fruit in his mouth. He spent a few minutes munching his way through this delicacy before commencing the long haul up the tree trunk, back into the hidden world way above my head. Quite why he came down to eat was a mystery. He had been sitting in a tree for the past sixty hours, feeding on the very same fruit. This one appeared to be no different to the rest but, obviously, the orang-utan felt it essential to eat it on the ground. No matter how long I work with animals, they will never cease to surprise me.

Durians are the orang-utans' favourite food and, on the assumption that more than twenty thousand intelligent, sentient apes cannot be wrong, I felt obliged to find out what the fuss was all about. It was one of the biggest mistakes of my life. I have experienced some truly offensive meals on my travels; deeply abhorrent food to make your toes curl in disgust. But nothing – nothing at all – prepared me for the smell of a durian. The fruit itself looks like a spiny melon and gives no external hints of the horrors lurking inside. Try to imagine a dustbin, full to the brim of the usual detritus produced by an average household and its kitchen. Imagine, then, that this bin has been sitting out in the warm sun for six weeks. Picture, if you will, a passer-by opening the lid, lowering his head and breathing deeply the powerful aroma that surges upward. That gives just the merest idea of the appalling stench produced by a ripe durian. The fruit itself may possibly have an acceptable taste but it is impossible to get through that initial physical trauma of the rank fetor. Orang-utans might be one of our closest relatives but I am deeply relieved that we don't share the same diet.

This trip had been planned for months; back in England I had lain in bed at night imagining the thrill of watching and working with wild orang-utans. But after four days of following this male my mind started to drift to new horizons. It was only when I found myself thinking, unbidden, of warm showers or my next project that I realised humans are pitifully fickle. The initial excitement was wearing thin, the male had only moved about three hundred metres and for most of the time he had been out of sight, masked by the leaves. Occasionally a shaggy foot or elbow hove into view for a millisecond but the shy ape was soon aware of his indiscretion and the peeping appendage was quickly pulled back into the canopy.

By this time I had taken less than a single roll of film, a woefully low tally that could have been bagged in a few seconds with a less introverted animal. I had been commissioned by a publisher to write and illustrate a book on the great apes; chimps, gorillas, bonobos and orang-utans. I had to take the pictures, write a text of 65,000 words and get the finished material to the publishers within a tight deadline. The trip to Indonesia was just one of several to squeeze in; time was an ever-present consideration that ultimately controlled every project.

The choice of illustrations in a wildlife book is hugely important, most people decide whether or not to buy a book within the first few seconds of picking it up. If the photographs are attractive and interesting, the book is likely to be successful. One of the keys to my job is to gather a wide and appealing set of pictures. Hairy, orange squares of miscellaneous anatomy sticking out from distant cracks in the canopy were not quite fulfilling this requirement. The chapter on orang-utans had to show more than mature males sitting in trees; if the book was going to sell it needed females, adolescents and – most of all – cute and cuddly babies. It was time to move on and find more orang-utans.

Over the next five days Joaquin took the boat further and further upstream. We stopped often to explore interesting looking parts of the forest and slowly my collection of orang-utan photographs grew. All of the sightings were brief and always the result of luck. I just happened to be in right place when the apes showed themselves. I found more males and even some adult females, which was very fortunate as they can go for literally months without coming down from the treetops. For once the gods were smiling on me.

Life in the boat was surprisingly comfortable. The food was dull and repetitive but then it often is on these trips. Joaquin obviously felt that, as a paying guest, I should have a degree of privacy. He slept at the back of boat, behind the wheelhouse, while I had the centre. My sleeping place was under the khlotok's wooden roof; there were no sides to this structure, just hefty corner posts to hold up the thick, heavy planks. A mosquito net hung down over the sleeping bag and, once inside, I could see and hear the forest all around without being pestered by the clouds of insects that droned above the sluggish river.

The sun went down at about seven o'clock. You will hardly be surprised to learn that there is little in the way of evening entertainment in a rainforest in the middle of Borneo, so at the risk of sounding dull I am forced to admit that, after eating, I just went to bed and read by torchlight. This isn't as turgidly uninteresting as it sounds. Forests have sharply delineated routines: at dusk the animals that make up the day shift retire to their sleeping grounds, while the nocturnal set of animals begins to stir, before venturing out into the darkness. Although nothing can be seen in the lowering gloom, the changeover in wildlife is unmistakable because of the completely new set of sounds they produce. A rainforest in daylight is dominated by birdsong, at night this is replaced by the call of frogs and toads: calls that bear no resemblance to the unimaginative croak of the frogs heard in English gardens. Frogs in Borneo produce a wonderful cacophony of squeals and squeaks, whistles and groans; some delivered at Morse-code speed – a string of clipped yaps that are over in a matter of seconds. Others communicate with languid, long moans that sound just like lazy yawns. These alien noises emanated from animals defending their own corner of the forest and advertising for potential mates. The pitch range of the calls spread across several octaves; on paper this might sound like a horrible discordant noise but the overall effect was truly eloquent and soporific. It was a delight to drift off to sleep against a lullaby of amorous amphibians announcing their territorial rights to the listening world.

Some of the most exhilarating moments took place at dawn. I have never needed an alarm clock in the morning; for some unknown reason my metabolism wakes automatically at six o'clock and has done so for years. This mechanism didn't fail me even on a steadily rocking longboat on the Indonesian river. I woke every day at six and lay listening to the sounds of the forest rhythms changing from nocturnal to diurnal. As the first rays of the sun showed themselves, the frogs slowly quietened, then the early birds began to sing and then for a few minutes all hell broke lose.

Sharing the orang-utans' habitat were a group of closely related animals called gibbons. These are true rain-forest specialists that hardly ever come to the ground. Gibbons are perfectly designed to travel at break-neck speed by swinging from branch to branch, clinging on with powerful hands that act just like grappling hooks. They live in tightly knit family groups that each own a strictly defined patch of forest. Gibbons re-enforce their ownership credentials through noise. Every morning the group gathers in the centre of their territory and gives out a song designed to remind all nearby gibbons that this area of the woodland is taken – so keep out. The male starts the set piece with a series of low whooping calls, then the females and youngsters join in, adding much higher voices to the ritual. The chorus quickly builds into an awesome crescendo, an irrepressible wave of sound that floods the forest in all directions, quelling budding invasions before they begin. Any neighbouring band of gibbons that might be planning a take-over would get the unequivocal message that this particular stretch of woodland was spoken for and that its rightful owners were fit, healthy and ready to repel intruders. The daily ceremony took place all around the forest, each group making a contribution to an irresistible early morning reveille. The gibbons' salute marked the beginning of every working day.

By keeping rough notes of the photographs accumulating in my box of used films, there came a point when it seemed I probably had enough pictures of adult orang-utans. Authors and publishers have long known that photographs of baby animals are a vital ingredient in all wildlife books. Humans are genetically programmed to be interested and protective towards the young of our own species. And, because primates are so closely related to us, few people are immune to the appeal of a wide-eyed infant ape; I had to get some pictures.

Orang-utan babies are particularly attractive. They are born with very little hair, which makes them appear even more human-like. They have small heads and wide, liquid-brown eyes that can melt a heart at a single glance. But the orang-utan's most potent weapon is, without doubt, its wonderful facial expression. I once heard a baby orang-utan described as having a face 'like a surprised coconut', and it is impossible to improve that description. The perpetual mask of astonished puzzlement worn by a young orang-utan makes it one of the world's most photogenic creatures. I wanted my book to be stuffed full of their portraits.

By now you will probably have guessed that I am about to add that taking these pictures wouldn't be easy. Young orang-utans face a long list of potential predators; they live in a forest brimming with large skilled hunters that are very partial to a meal of tender young primate. Female orang-utans are well aware of the risk to their young and avoid most of the dangers by taking the simple precaution of staying in the treetops, where the biggest carnivores cannot reach them. Baby orang-utans are born in the canopy, on carefully constructed nests woven into high, strong branches. At first they cling limpet-like to their mother as she clambers through the forest, but they soon hone their climbing skills. Even when the infant can make its own way around, the wily female takes care to keep the vulnerable youngster in the trees; most do not come down to the forest floor until they are almost a year old.

I needed young orang-utans that were more co-operative and this is where my weeks of research paid off. High on my list of destinations was a visit to an orang-utan rehabilitation centre just a few miles upstream. Although it was an essential stop, this place filled me with dread. It was not going to be a comfortable stay. Sadly some baby orang-utans pay dearly for their inherited charisma, because they are in great demand as pets. Orang-utans, as an endangered species, are covered by an international agreement that forbids anyone to buy or sell them without a hefty wad of official paperwork and permits. These are rarely granted, and only then to reputable organisations that know how to care for apes and can house them in precisely the right conditions.

But there are always people who conveniently overlook these laws for their own ends; young orang-utans can be sold for hard cash, so illicit traders ignore the licensing system and simply go into the forest and catch them. The truly sickening part of this trade stems from the fact that female orang-utans are careful, conscientious mothers that will defend their babies to the death. And that is exactly what many do. Poachers looking for infant apes in the forest are well aware that any nearby female orang-utan will climb high up and hide in the canopy as soon as she sees a human. There is only one way to capture a live baby orang-utan and that is to kill the mother before she has time to escape.

When the poacher spots a female carrying a baby he has a few seconds to strike before she disappears. The idea is to shoot the adult and miss the baby. This works maybe half the time; in the other attempts the youngster is killed at the same time as its mother. Even if the baby is unscathed by the bullet it runs a real risk of being crushed by its mother's body as she crashes from the treetops onto the hard ground beneath. Very few baby orang-utans are taken live from the corpse of their mother. Which is just as well, because those that die are the lucky ones.

A young orang-utan taken from the forest does not legally exist, therefore it can't be transported in the usual way. So it is locked into a wooden box marked sewing machines or souvenirs, and then shipped around like an unfeeling piece of furniture. At this stage the baby is severely traumatised; its mother is dead, the infant is alone for the first time in its life and has been mauled by one of its most formidable, terrifying enemies, Man. Many of the babies never reach their destination; they die of shock or dehydration. The few that ever reach the black market can expect a short and brutal life. They are sold to bar owners, travelling showmen or anyone who can use them to earn money. The terrified young animal is given the wrong sort of food and kept chained to a tabletop or locked in a mesh cage. Its miserable existence does not last long, because baby orang-utans always grow bigger. By the time it reaches seven years old the ape has developed into a powerful creature, and has been on the receiving end of appalling treatment that has made it profoundly fear and hate humans. Sooner or later it lashes out and attacks someone; with huge, flat, grinding teeth even an adolescent orang-utan can inflict a terrible bite. This act of desperation becomes the animal's death sentence. It can't be sold to a zoo because its has no licence – it doesn't exist. So the animal simply vanishes, buried somewhere with a bullet through its head – only to be replaced with another, dragged in along the same vile route.

Orang-utans have been exploited this way for a long time but very gradually the situation is improving. Even now babies are still being taken from the forest and sold, but an ever-increasing number of these will be rescued. Attitudes are changing to conservation; when these abused youngsters are seen by passers-by there is a good chance the owners will be reported and their animals confiscated by the police. We can only hope that this brings an end to such a disgusting trade.

Confiscation is obviously not the end of the story for the young apes. They are by now just five or six years old and have maybe another thirty-five years of life in front of them. The Indonesian authorities long ago decided that, instead of condemning them to spend the next few decades in a zoo, the animals should be given a second chance of living wild. Almost all rescued orang-utans are immediately shipped back to Borneo or Sumatra and taken to rehabilitation camps. These are remote areas of woodland where the apes have the opportunity of learning to survive independently, once they have recovered from their terrible experience at the hands of man.

The centres are permanently staffed by rangers whose job is to teach the apes how to look after themselves. This may sound absurd but a newly arrived adolescent orang-utan has no idea of life in the forest. He last saw it possibly four years earlier and since then has lived exclusively in a nightclub in Taiwan or a shed in a suburban garden. The forest is mysterious and alien; at first the animal can be unwilling to explore the menacing and unfamiliar habitat. Often he will not venture anywhere near the trees, and has to be coaxed or carried in. This is often difficult because a badly abused youngster is just as frightened of the human rangers as he is of the forest. It is a slow business but gradually the orang-utan tentatively explores its natural home; he learns to find food and regain his neglected climbing skills. The ultimate aim is to allow the orang-utans to return to the wild, but each animal has its own history and comes burdened with a unique set of problems. Success is not guaranteed.

There was a small rehabilitation centre not far away and this was about the only place where I could see youngsters at close range. These centres are, understandably, often closed to visitors; I had arranged a special permit while back in England and was already aware of the strict rules that governed outsiders in this sensitive place. The khlotok glided alongside an ancient, short jetty that led the way to a few wooden buildings. From the boat I could see three young orang-utans scattered around the clearing. One was eating, another was in a tree and the remaining animal sat on the ground with head bowed low and long arms curled around in a tight self-hug.

As I stepped from the boat two of the apes were unmoved by the intrusion; they ignored me totally. The third, still hugging himself, watched closely as I walked along the jetty; he then stood and shuffled off behind the largest of the wooden huts. Just then one of the rangers appeared and introduced himself. He was a gracious host and offered a guided tour before leaving me to my own devices. He showed me the record centre, which stores the known history of all the animals that had ever been through the camp. As we sifted through the sad chronicles of more than a hundred apes, I spotted the hugging orang-utan sitting on the roof of a small building across the clearing. We dug out his record card and read his story, a tale that was typically depressing.

He had been discovered by a tourist wandering through a market. The observant visitor was casually looking for souvenirs when he noticed a small wooden box rocking to and fro under a stall. It was a baby orang-utan locked inside a cage that was too small even to allow him to stand up. The stallholder, inevitably, claimed he had only bought the animal that morning, from someone he had never met before. The ape was confiscated and finally ended up in the rehabilitation centre. Physically he was in reasonable condition but deep inside he still bore the psychological scars of whatever barbarous treatment had left him wedged in a box under a market stall. He would eat but showed no interest in the forest. The ranger explained that the animal had only been in camp for about two weeks and many often took much longer to take advantage of their unfamiliar freedom.

Each orang-utan had its own history. One male had sores around his neck where a metal collar had been fitted when he was young; but as he got bigger the collar became tighter and eventually had to be sawn off to save his life. Another had his right arm missing – blown off by the same blast that killed his mother. One female had arrived a few days earlier, she had been rescued from a nightclub, not a moment too soon. No-one knew her exact background but she had been terribly treated; all around her back and shoulders were cigarette burns inflicted for fun or punishment. Even from a distance I could clearly see the round wounds that had taught her to be deeply terrified of humans. The three-year-old infant would not even eat if a ranger was anywhere nearby. No-one had yet managed to pick her up. Most of the time it is a privilege to work in these remote wildernesses with rare and endangered animals. But that morning my enjoyment evaporated; the only remaining emotion was a deep shame of my own species. The young orang-utans had been brought to this dreadful condition by sadistic, grasping humans that see wildlife as simply another natural resource to exploit and discard.

I found it difficult to stay in a place that was a constant reminder of the darker side of human nature but there was an encouraging light at the end of the tunnel. The centre had been open for more than fifteen years and had handled a small army of orang-utans; so far I had only seen the new arrivals. Further back in the forest were the old-hands, animals that had started to become independent. They had long ago recovered from whatever wounds and traumas had brought them here, and were now mastering the complex business of jungle survival. These were the

Baby orang-utans positively ooze charisma and appeal

apes I had come to see.

It took a while to find them; some were now completely at home in the forest and had wandered many miles from camp. They only returned out of curiosity or to pinch a few of the bananas the rangers left out for the less self-reliant orang-utans. There were plenty around but I still had to locate them. Over the next four days I wandered the forest and came across a wide variety of juvenile apes, ranging from energetic five year-olds to massive ten-year-olds on the verge of adulthood. Some still retained the memory of their treatment at the hands of humans and would disappear as soon as they were aware of me. Others, presumably less badly scarred, were indifferent. I followed these through the forest, taking photographs and marvelling at the way they had made the transition from captivity to a wild existence. Soon I had enough pictures of youngsters to satisfy even the most demanding editor. I went back to camp to thank the staff before going back to work with the truly wild orang-utans.

As I walked into the clearing, a tiny orang-utan loped over and locked herself onto my left ankle. She clung on with a grip like a vice; orang-utans are solid, well-built creatures, this one may have only been young but she was impressively heavy. Walking with this living ball-and-chain was impossible so I sat down on a nearby log. Looking down I could clearly see a series of circular bald patches. This was the young female that had been tortured with cigarettes. The burns had probably destroyed the follicles and hair would never again grow on these scars. Immediately the ape released her grip and started climbing up my leg. Typical of her species, she was methodically slow, hand over hand she pulled herself up, propelled from behind by short strong legs. Without hesitation the orang-utan pushed her head into my shirt, climbed inside, wrapped her long arms around my back and promptly went to sleep.

Since I had last seen her, the rangers had spent hours carefully convincing the ape that not all humans are cruel monsters; some can even be trusted. She had learned the lesson surprisingly quickly. At her age, in the wild, this infant would still be with her mother. Orang-utans usually have just one baby and they invest all of their time and care into its survival. Until the fatal shot, this tiny female would have slept with her mother, travelled and eaten with her mother; the two would have been inseparable. The youngster would have carefully watched the adult, gradually absorbing the knowledge she needed to survive. The baby had missed all of this company and affection and was in desperate need of comfort from a warm, large animal. That day it was my turn to be mum. The vulnerable ape lay inside my T-shirt and revelled in the sort of close contact that had been murderously cut short by a poacher. It was an extraordinarily moving moment; when the baby finally woke and slid down to the ground, I knew that this brief contact had been just as important to me as it had been to the orang-utan.

After 'How on earth do you manage to get close enough to a wild animal to take a picture?' the question most heard by wildlife photographers is 'Aren't you frightened of all those animals? Lions, tigers, crocodiles and snakes – aren't you worried that they might attack you?'

To be frank, if I thought that lions, tigers, crocodiles and snakes were really going to attack me, like any rational person I would be worried to the point of screaming hysteria. But they don't. It is extremely difficult to stalk an animal close enough to take a picture; they see us coming and make a beeline for the distant horizon. The few that are not frightened simply want to be left alone; as long as we keep a respectful distance from them, there are no problems. Strange as it may seem, I am not at all worried about the big animals, it is the small ones that terrify me.

I am not an entomologist and know very little about creepy-crawlies. I could only put a name to a tiny number of the teeming bugs that swarmed through the forests of Borneo. Army ants, scorpions, mosquitoes, strange brown things with lots of legs, slimy green creatures that hung on the underside of leaves, a monstrous yellow striped flying beast that looked like a cross between a wasp and a turkey; the list could go on forever. They may all have been different shapes and sizes but they had one thing in common – they were out to get me. It's never the big animals that cause trouble, it's the small ones. Even with a barrier of industrial strength insect-repellent that could, quite literally, melt plastic, the bugs managed to break through my defences. There were creepy-crawlies in my socks, nestling in my armpits, in my ears and in places where no truly respectable insect would ever wish to be found.

After three weeks in the rainforest my clothes could probably stand up by themselves. I smelt like a yak's armpit. A drifting raft of unidentifiable miscellaneous debris formed a deeply unattractive blanket across the entire width of the river. A wash in this water would have been completely pointless; I would have come out even dirtier than before, having contracted at least two diseases previously unknown to science. I was bone-tired, hungry, had aches and pains in the few places that were still capable of feeling. I was covered in bites and was almost certain that something was living in my beard – and people have the nerve tell me how lucky I am to do this for a living. And the problems don't stop there.

A few days before leaving for Borneo I had given a talk at a primary school back home in Shropshire, and during the question time one of the children had put up her hand and asked 'Why is a rain forest called a rain forest? Does it make rain?' Children sometimes have an instinctive knack of cutting to the heart of the matter. For those of you that have ever thought of posing that same question, rain forests have earned their name simply because it rains – an incredible amount. It rains almost every day; not wishy-washy, effete British rain but uncompromising, macho rain that blocks out the sight and sound of the surrounding world with its power. Rain even more impressive than that found in Scotland. From the sky fall fat, heavy raindrops that can cause physical pain as they hit. I was in Borneo during the dry season, which sounds as if it should be reasonably comfortable. But the terms 'dry season' and 'wet season' must have been coined by someone with a whimsical sense of humour; they are relative terms that are not to be understood literally. In a rainforest you are never far away from a soaking, it is just a matter of degree. During the dry season it rains a lot; the dry season is, in fact, wet. But just not quite as sodden as the wet season, which is amazingly, ridiculously, offensively wet.

Rainforests are hot and humid the whole time; it is a little like living in a sauna. This causes hygienic problems. An unwary traveller, after a week in the forest, may take off his socks one day to find a mysterious growth blooming between his toes. This is one of the richest habitats on earth; seeds and spore drift through the air trying to find somewhere damp to set up home. Most desirable locations have already been claimed; a human body is not a bad alternative if all of the conventional spots are occupied. Invading flora can be a very real risk, if you don't keep clean. It was time for a shower and a change of clothes.

A few miles downstream was a riverside lodge, a sort of minimalist rainforest hotel. For just a few dollars I could spend a comfortable night in a bed, get clean and wash some clothes. The thought was alluring; suddenly I couldn't wait and asked Joaquin to head for this oasis. The lodge was a collection of small huts built in a clearing, completely surrounded by forest. Inevitably everything was made of wood: there is no other building material available in these parts. The compound was reached by a long jetty leading from the river to a huge entrance that looked rather oddly like a Swiss chalet. I checked in and was given an ice-cold bottle of mineral water. The single fridge was powered by electricity from a solar panel built into the roof. Intense sunshine, between the deluges, is one of the advantages of working in the tropics. The panels were small and only supplied a trickle of power, just enough to recharge batteries for the radio and keep the fridge cool. After days of drinking water that felt warmer than my own body temperature, ice was a gloriously self-indulgent pleasure.

My room was simply a small shed with a thatched roof; there were no glass windows, just wooden shutters. The bed was a revelation simply because it was a real bed, with a mattress and pillow. These were sybaritic luxuries after sleeping on the hard planks of a boat for so long. The lodge had a part-time cook and that evening she came in to prepare supper for Joaquin and me. There were no other guests staying, and we ate alone on a table overlooking the river, while fruit bats whirled overhead. The meal was a local dish called nasi goreng, a mixture of rice, vegetables and spices, steamed and served in a huge leaf tied with string. But more importantly it came with a huge bottle of ice-cold water.

Although there were two free beds, Joaquin opted to sleep on his boat, while I headed for the opulence of my room. I had already taken a shower, in water extracted from the river and cleaned through a very effective filter. The water was pumped into a tank perched precariously on the roof of my hut, and it was unheated. But the tanks are filled at dawn and the sun had been beating down on this small metal box for several hours, the shower spray emerged at a perfect temperature. But I can't help thinking that, just then, a shower of any temperature would have been perfect.

I climbed into a bed with crisp, clean sheets, and realised that humans don't really need too many twenty-first century gadgets to live well.

A reasonable meal, shower and decent bed were the stuff of dreams. Although there were no electric lights in my room, I prolonged the pleasure by reading in the faint glow of a pencil torch. Suddenly, from one of the unlit, distant, corners of my room, came the subdued but unmistakable sound of a burp. I had grown used to the strange noises seeping out from a nocturnal rainforest but this was completely new. It was polite and almost refined, but it was most definitely a burp and I was eager to find its source. With the torch I scanned the room, which didn't take long, as it was very small. I could see nothing that might have produced such an unlikely call. *Bu-urp* came the sound for the second time, and it appeared to come from a chunk of bark clinging to the wall next to the closed shutter. As the entire room was built of rough, unfinished planking, there were bits of rustic tree-trunk everywhere. Then this particular scrap of bark moved, dashed forward and then stopped. It could only be one thing – a gecko, one of my favourite creatures on earth.

Geckos are lizards with a unique talent for climbing vertical surfaces. They are designed for life in the forests, where they skulk high in the trees searching for insects, but the special feet that allow them to climb tree trunks also enable these reptiles to cling onto man-made walls and even ceilings. They are completely harmless and should be welcomed into bedrooms because they eat many of the insects that are far less amiable. I had seen geckos in many other places but never one that made a noise before. A burping gecko: this was an Edward Lear-like creation that wouldn't be out of place in the pea-green boat along with the owl and the pussycat.

The gecko, like almost every other inhabitant of the forest, was simply telling potential rivals to keep out. It was that rarest of sounds: a territorial burp. As I watched he darted forward again to seize a bright orange spider that had just emerged from a crack in the planking. He swallowed the wriggling creature, stuck out his disconcertingly long tongue and licked his eyes slowly and deliberately; he then gave out a burp of satisfaction and sprinted into the darkness of a remote corner.

Delighted to share my room with such a surreal creature, I went back to bed and switched off the torch. As my light went off the fireflies switched themselves on. In the pitch black of my room, tiny males declared their prowess with an intense brilliant light designed to impress passing females. Each fly darted around the room, invisible apart from the glowing advert coming from its tail. There must have been about twenty of these creatures floating around; they reminded me of the still fiery flecks that sometimes rise skyward from bonfires. At first their movements seemed random but then I realised that each light carefully kept away from the others. They all needed their own space in which to shine. I got out of bed again, to try to see the creatures themselves and as I groped for the torch in the darkness, the diminutive lights went out as if the power had failed. A few seconds later they returned, but would vanish again at the slightest sound.

One of the problems of advertising your presence so clearly is that predators, as well as females, can see exactly where you are. The male fireflies had to carefully balance survival with the need to attract a mate. As females make no noise, whenever the males heard a sound, it couldn't be a mate but it might be something more menacing, so they turned off their beacons until the danger passed. Fascinatingly, they totally ignored the sounds of the burping gecko. They somehow knew that lizards are confined to the walls and cannot reach food that is still in mid-air. I watched the fireflies dancing and listened to the geckos burping; little did I know this was to be my last night in the Bornean rainforest.

10

Legwork

J ust a few minutes after dawn, while still struggling to wake, I felt the bed begin to shake. It was just a dull vibration at first, as if a lorry was driving too close to the hut, but it quickly became a lot more intense and the bed began to slide towards the door. Clouds of dust and twigs fell from the flimsy thatched roof opening up a narrow hole to the deep blue sky. The earthquake wasn't particularly dramatic or violent but the unexpected shuddering of the walls made the panic-stricken geckos scuttle for cover. The sun's first light had just appeared over the eastern horizon prompting the gibbons' daily hooting ritual. This started as a relatively low-key performance with just a few animals calling but gradually each member of the family added its voice. But the troop was not allowed to perform its usually impressive repertoire. Half way through the overture, the trees that supported the howling apes began to rock and sway. As the whole forest floor shuddered the gibbons stopped mid-hoot, before reaching their normal screaming crescendo. The earthquake lasted about twelve seconds and subsided into a short series of minor grumbling after-shocks.

Above the canopy small flocks of fruit bats circled the sky; they had not long ago returned to their day-roosts after a night combing the woods for ripe fruit. The swaying branches had disturbed their sleep and, in the unfamiliar brilliance of dawn, they wheeled in confusion when they should have been hanging upside down in the cool shade of a giant tree. For the next ten minutes there was complete silence. I could picture the animals sitting around in a state of stunned disbelief, unable to comprehend what had happened to their world for a few moments. Then out on the river a single broadbill began its plaintive whistles; this seemed to be a signal to the other birds that life still went on. Tentative calls rang out and soon the forest returned to its early morning ritual of song. But for today only the gibbons had retired early; rudely interrupted before bringing their performance to its hysterical climax, they stubbornly refused to start again.

At the time the earthquake was just an interesting diversion; I had felt worse at home in England and soon forgot about it. Twenty minutes later I had breakfast sitting on a wooden floating pontoon overlooking the river. This first meal of the day was always my favourite. The sun was still quite low and the temperature was comfortable; ideal conditions for tucking into small hard-boiled eggs, a pile of unpeeled mixed fruits and a plastic mug of black coffee. Indonesia produces some of the finest coffee in the world and it was a wonderfully hedonistic experience to drink it, freshly roast and ground, while watching the portly proboscis monkeys lumbering around the trees on the far side of the river. Unlike the other primates, proboscis monkeys never look as if they have any fun. Squirrel monkeys and vervets are always busy doing something; they chase each other, scamper around the trees and investigate anything remotely interesting. But proboscis monkeys appear to have a terribly serious, almost puritanical, approach to life. They seem to have an important mission, which must be achieved at all costs, and, whatever this may be, it leaves no time for play.

Joaquin always joined me for breakfast, to discuss the plans for the day, but this morning he was not a happy man.

'Miker, Miker the earthshake has brought down many trees, the river is blocked. The boat cannot move today.'

Joaquin slept on his khlotok, which was moored just around a bend in the river. He enjoyed his privacy and stayed away from the main camp. Cushioned by the water, he had hardly noticed the vibrations of the quake, but he couldn't fail to notice the giant trees as they crashed from the banks and fell across the river. Trees in tropical rainforests have very shallow root systems; water is easily accessible and they do not need to send down the long tap roots needed by trees in drier parts of the world. A massive oak in a European forest is securely anchored by tough old roots that penetrate many metres into the soil below; it almost becomes part of the land itself and can withstand a savage battering from a gale. Trees in a rain forest are not equipped with these foundations and can be knocked down with surprisingly little force. The earthquake disturbed roots all along the riverbank; dozens of trees lost their flimsy grip in the earth and toppled. They could not fall backward or sideways because the forest around was too densely packed. There was only one way to go, so they dropped into the open space of the river. And now, as far we could see in both directions, trees of all sizes lay across the water like a row of fallen dominoes. There would be no river traffic that day or for some time to come.

My flight to London was due in just two days' time. Usually it would take about twenty-two hours to reach Jakarta, but suddenly the quick route out of the forest had been well and truly blocked. Chain saws are expensive and rare tools in central Borneo, they are the exclusive property of professional loggers and the closest timber camp was twenty miles upstream. The giant trees had to be dissected by hand, a colossal task that would involve everyone in the village. The river was a lifeline for the people of the forest and it was essential that the blockage be cleared as soon as possible.

Work began immediately. Men were organised in teams, some on boats and others crawling along the fallen trunks. Using small axes and ancient saws they started to dismember the trees. Timber from tropical rainforest is not called hardwood without reason. Most of the treetrunks were unbelievably tough; all but the mightiest axe blow rebounded viciously and left only a tiny scar. It was like trying to cut down a concrete pillar. Axes and saws soon became blunt in this very uneven battle. Children ferried saws and axes to the bank, where women sharpened the blades and sent them back to the sweating men who were making little impression on the iron-hard logs. Joaquin was completely relaxed about the whole matter. He had seen it happen before and he would again.

'We must wait Miker. Three days maybe four. The river will soon be clear.'

I had complete faith in Joaquin's prediction, but it was of little comfort. I was due to give a prestigious and lucrative lecture in Cambridge, the day after getting back to England. The journey to Jakarta had to start that day but the boat was trapped, marooned by fallen trees. With Joaquin as interpreter I spoke to the village elders and, on their advice, reluctantly decided that the only possible way out was on foot. Most settlements in Borneo are built close to the river; water is the main highway of the forest and, in theory, it should be easy to walk downstream until the river became clear then hire a local boat from the nearest village to take me out of the forest.

My equipment went easily into a rucksack; carbon fibre cameras are amazingly lightweight, and the most vulnerable gadgets were wrapped in clothes for protection. A bottle of drinking water was the only heavy part of the luggage. I had chartered Joaquin and his boat for another two days, but now he was stranded at the lodge, unable to get home. He had become a good friend over the past weeks and had taught me a lot about Indonesian culture and folklore. Working exclusively with wild animals is time-consuming and leaves few opportunities to explore the other wonders of the world. Finding a local boatman with a true mastery of English had been a wonderful stroke of luck; I had enjoyed Joaquin's company and was sorry to desert him in such a predicament. As we said our goodbyes, Joaquin revealed that his wife had a cousin nearby; he could stay here until the river was cleared. We shook hands, and from an ancient hessian bag, he produced a huge palm of bananas and handed them to me saying, 'these will feed you on your trip back to the city.'

He then took out a hand-axe from the boat's toolbox and joined the teams hacking through the trees. I carefully wrapped the bananas in my towel and packed them into the rucksack.

Joaquin had said that there were villages every few miles along the riverbank. Reaching them would be simple, but he had no way of knowing how much of the river downstream would be blocked by trees. I began the walk about two hours after dawn. Rain forests in adventure stories are always too melodramatic. After watching a Hollywood movie it is easy to believe that snakes drip from every branch while huge man-eating cats lurk in the shadows waiting for unsuspecting victims. This image might fill cinemas but the less exciting truth is that, although rain forests are one of the richest habitats on earth, there is not much to see. Wild animals look on humans as the ultimate predator and avoid us at all costs. Acute senses warn them of our presence long before we get close.

The local tribespeople are skilled and silent when moving through the forest, but outsiders are usually noisy and clumsy. They advertise their presence loudly and the wildlife around has plenty of time to escape without being seen. There was really no danger from marauding animals during my quick hike.

Newcomers to a rainforest are always struck by just how gloomy it is inside. Tropical forests have an incredible and unique architecture; it is almost like being in a vast cathedral. Everything is on a huge scale, and the silence is overwhelming. Enormous tree trunks seem to be sculptured pillars that support a vaulted, leafy roof shrouded in impenetrable shadow. Visibility is low due to the sheer number of trees and, anyway, there is not much to see at ground level. The richest growth is in the canopy, the highest layer of the forest, where sunlight falls. So the vast majority of forest birds stay in the treetops feeding on fruit, nuts and insects. Only five percent of sunlight penetrates the thick layer of leaves to reach the ground; the forest floor is dark and silent. Underfoot there is virtually no greenery, because there is no sunshine to produce growth.

The floor is made up of rotting leaves and branches which build up into a thick soft layer over the years. The only visible animals are those insects that eat decaying vegetation or each other. Ants of all shapes and sizes scurry around and strange scorpion-like insects sit on the skeletal remains of leaves and freeze whenever they detect movement. Very occasionally there is a chink in the canopy and an intense beam of light floods a patch of the forest floor. Here islands of thick green vegetation spring up, but the growth comes to a well-defined end where the narrow spotlight of sunshine melts into the forest shadow. For a while there is a race upwards: tree seeds that have lain dormant for years, waiting for such an opportunity, suddenly sprout and grow at a phenomenal rate. Under these conditions the winner takes all. The first tree to reach the canopy quickly spreads its branches to fill the gap; those smaller saplings left beneath will then be starved of sunlight and soon wither in the gloom.

By following the river downstream, I couldn't possibly get lost. Apart from the relentless insects the trip was quick and uneventful until early afternoon. It was then that I realised the ground was becoming increasingly boggy; this soon gave way to a huge lake of shallow, murky water. The main river was fed by hundreds of small streams that drained the forest, but in the dry season these should have slowed down to thin trickles. A few minutes later the cause of the flood became obvious. Just ahead, on its side, lay a truly gargantuan tree whose roots had once formed part of the river bank. When the giant had been felled by the earthquake, it ripped out a large chunk of the bank creating a breach that allowed the water to seep into the forest.

At first I tried to go around but the pool was already too large and was still growing; there was just not enough time left to find an easier route. I stuck to the original plan and kept close to the riverbank, walking through the flood. At its deepest the water was no more than ankle height but there are disturbing hazards associated with water in the tropics. It took less than an hour to cross the flood and, once out of it, I rolled up my trousers expecting the worst. Three leeches had squirmed in and attached themselves firmly to my legs. These creatures are a frequent nuisance in rain forests but I have never managed to get used to them. The sight of a blood-bloated leech clinging to my flesh still sends shivers down my spine. The first reaction of most people is to pull them off, but this can be dangerous as the sucking mouthparts are usually left under the skin and can cause nasty infections. The only safe way of dealing with a leech is to persuade it to release its hold. This can be done simply by squeezing its tail very hard or by sprinkling a little salt over the animal. Once the leech has dropped off, the wound bleeds profusely for quite a while afterwards. The leech incorporates an anticoagulant in its bite, which prevents clotting and makes the blood flow freely so that the animal can easily feed. It is not a pleasant experience, but worse was to come.

The first two villages downstream had also been cut off by earthquake debris. But it didn't take long to reach a wider stretch of river where, although trees were down, there was enough open water to allow boats to squeeze past. By late afternoon I reached a third village and there, moored at an old wooden jetty, was the water-boat. This may sound like a childish name but the water-boat is not only a boat that goes on the water, it is also a boat that carries water.

The 'black rivers' of Indonesia are some of the most unhealthy waterways on earth. They are fine for washing clothes and even bathing, as long as you're careful not to swallow any during the process and never swim with an open wound. But for cooking and drinking, river water in Borneo poses a real health risk. Thanks to an increasingly comprehensive education programme, health awareness, even in the forest, is considerably more sophisticated than thirty years ago. The waterboat was a relatively new scheme that supplied clean water to remote villages, at a relatively low price. Every day the boat trundled along a different stretch of river taking healthy water to villages that had no supply of their own. The problems that had stopped my boat coming downriver had also prevented others going upstream and amongst those stranded was the waterboat. The antique craft couldn't go any further and was reluctantly turning around to head for home. After a long and confusing conversation with the captain, which involved pointing, mime and endless use of a phrasebook, he offered me a lift on the boat which was going all the way back to town.

Progress was agonisingly slow. The waterboat was another traditional Indonesian khlotok, a solid narrow workhorse of a vessel built for stamina rather than water skiing. We meandered along the river at walking pace. This was a purely functional craft, with no benches for passengers. I sat on one of the huge water barrels watching the forest slide by. Riverbanks are some of the best places to watch wildlife in the tropics. They mark the border between woodland and water, and are perfect spots to see animals from both worlds. Giant kingfishers perched on overhanging branches. European kingfishers are tiny creatures but these were the size of pigeons. Crocodiles sunbathed on exposed mud banks, but at the first sight of the boat they slipped silently into the black water, leaving barely a ripple.

Competition for sunlight is fierce amongst forest plants and, on the river, trees on both banks leaned into the gap above the water to grab more of the life-giving light. Some had grown such violent slants that it was not at all surprising they had toppled with the earthquake. They looked as if they couldn't have survived a strong wind. On narrow stretches, the bigger branches actually met over the river to form a cool, welcome tunnel of leaves.

The trip seemed endless and watching the unchanging green walls of the forest my mind started to wander. One of the penalties of travelling alone is that most of the time there is no-one to talk to: conversations and ideas take place internally. After several weeks in the forest, living on a diet

147

of stodgy rehydrated food, the occasional fish and some fruit, my mind as always turned to food. By now blood sugar levels were low and my body longed for something – anything – sweet. My usual remedy for this condition is chocolate; I always take several chunky bars carefully stashed in the luggage. But in the tropics chocolate turns into a mushy, sticky soup that attracts ants and provides a growing medium for all kinds of mysterious fungi. Sadly none was packed for this trip.

In my teens, before ever setting foot on foreign soil, I had devoured travel and adventure books. Other travellers had written about their desire for sugar so the feeling came as no surprise. Sitting on a khlotok drifting through the rivers of Borneo, I was living the kind of adventures that had fascinated me from childhood. Rain forests, crocodiles, earthquakes and even leeches were the stuff of my young fantasies. Perhaps I should put pen to paper like my early heroes. But, in my heart of hearts, I must humbly admit to a terrible handicap. Other travel writers had wonderfully evocative names that perfectly fitted their trade. Laurens van der Post and Wilfred Thesiger, these were glorious swashbuckling names that looked good in press releases and reviews. Redmond O'Hanlon – now that was a name to conjure up images of daring deeds and groundbreaking exploration. But my name was a serious drawback. *Alone in a Bornean Jungle* by Michael …… It simply didn't work. My parents should have had the foresight, the common decency, to call me Charlton or Monroe, something that would look suitably dashing on a dustcover. This was an insoluble problem that I have been forced to live with and accept with resignation.

We had only been travelling a short time when the boat pulled in to a ramshackle jetty built alongside a dozen small huts. The captain jumped off and started a noisy conversation with the nearest villager. After a few minutes, a long line of people formed, all carrying buckets and containers of every shape and size. Using a hand-operated pump the captain's mate filled each receptacle with water. The operation was slick and obviously practised; it took just twenty minutes to complete. A villager handed a bundle of money to the captain and we continued downstream. Two miles later we reached another village and the whole water unloading procedure was repeated. At the fifth stop, another bucket-bearing queue appeared and, at the back, was a familiar face. It was Wamena. He obviously did not expect to see a friend perched on top of the waterboat; it wasn't until I called out that he noticed me.

'Miker, what are you doing here?'

I explained about Joaquin's boat and the unscheduled lift on the water carrier.

'The waterboat only comes here once a week; it came just three days ago. The Captain couldn't sell the water upstream because the river was blocked and now he doesn't want to take his load back to town; he asks if we want to buy extra at half the usual price.'

The canny villagers were quick to seize this rare bargain; soon everyone had replenished their stocks at a very reasonable rate. The Captain had also salvaged something from the trip. Before we left I said goodbye to Wamena, and as I climbed back onto the boat, he said with a wicked grin,

'Next time the waterboat comes we give a lower price. The captain must make much profit if today he can sell at half the usual rate.'

The free enterprise culture was alive and thriving in Borneo.

The boat next stopped at a village very close to the rehabilitation centre I had visited earlier. This was where some rangers and their families lived, away from the main research buildings. The men from the water boat had some family here and took the opportunity to visit for a while. In a conversation that was a mixture of their broken English and my appalling Indonesian, I eventually got the message that we would not leave for at least another two hours. This gave me some free time to take another quick look at the rehabilitated orang-utans. The water-boat had a large dug-out canoe tied to the side and it was only a ten-minute paddle to reach the orang-utans, so I piled the cameras in and set off. Just then I remembered the bananas that Joaquin had given me earlier that day. I wrapped them in a waterproof plastic bag, added a few stones for weight, tied some string to the bag and dropped it into the river. Although the surface of the water was warm, the bottom of the river was much colder and ideal for cooling food. I arrived at the landing jetty of the rehabilitation centre, pulled up the bag and had lunch on the canoe. In the heavy, wet heat of the rainforest a chilled, fresh banana is one of the great joys of life.

As I started my second banana, a young male orang-utan strolled out of the forest at the far end of the jetty. It was the middle of the day and he was taking life easy. For a while he sat at the bottom of a tree. With huge fingers he plucked leaves from the lowest branches and delicately rolled them into narrow tubes before popping them into his mouth and chewing without much enthusiasm. He noticed me immediately but obviously wasn't particularly interested until the banana appeared. Orang-utans have very good eyesight and he soon realised that my meal was much more exciting than his. Like all apes, orang-utans adore bananas; they are one of their favourite foods. I had some and he didn't, so this unfair situation obviously had to be rectified. The optimistic ape wandered down the jetty and perched at the very end, trying to reach the boat with his great, sweeping arms. But the river current was strong and the canoe was being tugged downstream and was held only by straining ropes tied securely to tree trunks. Try as he might the orang-utan couldn't quite grab the boat. If this had been a chimpanzee, he would have exploded with rage. He would have screamed and stamped with frustration, his hair would have stood on end and he would probably have thrown stones at me for not helping. But orang-utans are much more relaxed about life; instead of throwing a tantrum he just sat calmly and watched me.

It sounds terribly callous to sit surrounded by bananas while a hungry orang-utan pleads with gentle brown eyes to join the feast. The temptation to feed him was almost unbearable but I knew the risks of giving him food. Orang-utans are a frighteningly endangered species and humans are their biggest enemy. This animal was already too comfortable in the presence of man; if I fed him he would learn to become even more friendly and this trust could be fatal if ever he met a human whose intentions were less amicable than mine.

Orang-utans are dark horses; to the casual observer they seem slow and lethargic but this woolly image masks a razor-sharp, original mind. After staring at me for a few minutes the ape turned around and wandered back along the jetty. This was an ancient structure that had seen better days. The wooden planks were warped and rotting, most of the nail heads had long since rusted. Walking along the jetty the orang-utan casually and discreetly tested each plank with his fingers; he wrapped his hand around the edge and gave a gentle tug upwards before letting go. Within a

minute he found exactly what he needed. At the first pull, the end of the plank came away from the thick beams that made up the skeleton of the jetty. Immediately he dropped onto his side and slid his whole hand underneath. The plank came up far enough to allow him to get his whole forearm under. An orang-utan arm is thicker than my leg; it was an uneven battle and as he pushed and pulled I could hear the scream of reluctant rusty nails giving up their hold in the wood. It took less than thirty seconds to tear it free. Like every wooden artefact in the forest, this plank had been cut by hand, probably with an old bow-saw. No two were the same size; the orang-utan had found a plank that was much bigger than a household floorboard in Britain. It was several centimetres thick and wide enough for two children to stand abreast. The ape dragged the plank to the end of the jetty and stood it up on end. He looked me in the eyes for a moment and then carefully lowered the plank, like a drawbridge, onto the side of boat. Orang-utans may be big and bulky but they spend most of their lives in the treetops, for such a colossal animal they are incredibly agile and confident climbers. Like a rampaging buccaneer the orang-utan crossed the plank and stormed my canoe. He slid into the boat, grabbed the remaining bananas, returned over the improvised bridge to the jetty and then disappeared into the forest with his booty.

I was truly stunned. That was, without doubt, the most intelligent action I had ever seen performed by an animal. Orang-utans don't normally raid boats by breaching them with planks. He had sat and presumably thought deeply about the problem and worked out a completely novel way of solving it. He was using his mind creatively. I have never been more impressed and, just to make me feel better about being robbed, he still retained his fear of humans. A tame ape would have stolen the bananas and stayed on the boat to eat them, this chap was too wary to feed in my company. With his imaginative brain and suspicion of humans this orang-utan obviously had a rosy future and I was delighted to donate my lunch to such a wonderfully inventive animal.

The waterboat finally dropped me off a whole day later than planned. By then my clothes crackled with dried mud from the swampy trek downstream, and my boots oozed with black slime. In the humidity of a Borneo river, I had accumulated sweat in a greasy sheen like a second skin from head to toe. Even to my desensitised nose I smelt worse than a proverbial pig; no airline would let me on board a long-haul flight in that condition. I changed into the one remaining cleanish set of clothes in the rucksack and had a quick wash on the boat. Using a local taxi and two short internal flights I reached Jakarta thirty hours after the plane, and my reserved seat, had already left for London. The airport at Jakarta is palatial; it has to be one of most impressive terminals in the world. I found the information desk and, surprisingly, the airline was very understanding about my predicament and quickly arranged a replacement ticket back to London. Unfortunately I had missed the direct flight and had to be re-routed on a series of short hops, changing at Singapore, Karachi, Abu Dhabi and Paris.

The flight left at ten o'clock the next morning. With a completely free night ahead I had just one thought in mind – a good hotel, clean bed and, more than anything else, a hot bath. The idea was appealing, and it was only one night after all, so I splashed out and booked into one of Jakarta's most luxurious hotels. After sleeping in the forest this was going to be a real pleasure. My room was completely over the top. It was equipped with three televisions, including one in the bathroom. The room service menu was the length of a short novel and made me giddy with anticipation. It contained all the usual culinary delights found in a top-notch hotel and, at the bottom, was a note that added,

'Not all items are listed. Please speak to Room Service Manager if you desire other commodities. We will endeavour to help.'

International hotels of this calibre are resourceful and do not like to be beaten. I telephoned the Room Service Manager and asked for a large bar of chocolate.

The Manager was completely unruffled.

'We'll do our best sir,' he told me; just asking for it made my mouth water. Half an hour later there was a gentle knock on the door. Outside stood a waiter carrying a small tray. On this, wrapped in a snow-white napkin, was a large box of real Belgian chocolates.

This was beyond my wildest dreams: the hotel had kept its pledge magnificently. I gave a handful of *rupiah* to the waiter and closed the door, aware that this was the perfect culmination to a very successful trip. Chocolate should be savoured in comfort I turned the bathtaps on full, switched on the television and sank into the decadent round tub full of hot water. As several layers of river slime soaked away and the indelicate odour of orang-utan disappeared I watched the news and caught up with world events that had unfolded during my stay in the forest.

The grime was deeply ground into the soles of my feet. They had spent just too many hours wading through murky swamps. I've always thought that human feet aren't wildly attractive at the best of times, and at that moment mine were particularly offensive. Polluted and giving off a very insanitary aroma, these feet required urgent attention. After a long soak, they still needed a scouring with a scrubbing brush. It was during the fifth truffle that I noticed a strange ceaseless rippling movement on the soft skin beneath the toenails. It looked just like the surface of a pond caught in a gentle breeze. This came as a surprise, as 'rippling' is an adjective that has never been applied to my physique.

A camera lens makes an excellent magnifying glass if you turn it around and look through the back. Sitting in the bath I minutely examined my toes and the exquisite Belgian chocolate suddenly lost its flavour. Just beneath my toenails were a series of tiny holes and, out of these, I could clearly see the tips of small white wriggly things, and they were all waving at me.

Having read a small library of reference books before going to Borneo, I knew exactly what had happened. Rainforests are home to a host of insects whose sole aim in life is to reproduce in incalculable numbers. Conscientious mothers are careful to lay their eggs close to a good food supply, so their offspring can eat and grow as soon as they hatch. During my march through the flooded forest one of these unspeakable, unidentified creatures had unobtrusively burrowed into my toes and laid its eggs. I knew all about this problem, but reading about it was a very different matter to finding the living maggots cavorting in my feet. My immediate response was a strong desire to amputate both legs at the knee; this was followed by an overwhelming sensation that the Belgian chocolates were about to make an unwelcome reappearance.

It's at times like this that I always regret not listening to my careers teacher at school. I could quite clearly remember his scathing condemnation of my ambition.

'Don't be stupid Leach. Of course you can't work with wild animals. There's no career structure, no job opportunities. You'll starve. Go away and come back with some more sensible ideas.'

Unfortunately I didn't listen and, just at that moment, deeply regretted my wayward decision. Suddenly accountancy or quantity surveying seemed far more attractive professions than mine. Lawyers' or dentists' feet never got eaten by bugs; this was an aspect of working with wildlife that I had obviously not fully thought out beforehand. The grubs were still small but they would grow horribly quickly and eventually gnaw their way free. I knew that this would be painful, but far worse was the thought that these creatures were growing fat at the expense of my body tissue. I am not normally a mean man but, after all, they were my toes and I wasn't ready to donate them to an unknown quantity of grubs. This really was the stuff of nightmares.

After the first wave of panic passed, I realised that direct action was needed if only to safeguard my sanity. Packed at the bottom of the luggage was a comprehensive first aid kit that would make some doctors envious.

It had been put together several years before and had never once been used; everything was still packed in pristine blister packs including the surgical scalpel.

It is probably best to draw a discrete veil over the exact details of the ad-lib surgery but, in rough terms, I opened the end of each toe with the scalpel and soaked both feet in a bowl of highly salted water. Even man-eating grubs have to breathe and, with their air holes underwater, they were eventually forced to abandon their homes and come up to the surface. The salty water helped disinfect the remaining carnage. Before going to bed, I closed the wounds with a strip of plaster. It was truly a miserable evening; I had dreamt of one leisurely comfortable night, feasting on chocolates in a luxurious hotel room. Instead it was spent with lacerated feet soaking in a bowl of bloodied water.

In the morning I realised that the next day just wasn't going to be any better. As soon as my feet touched the floor, I discovered that each toe had swollen to grotesque proportions. They were unbelievably sore and had grown to the size of plums; the puffy flesh threatened to engulf the toenails. The resemblance to a plum wasn't restricted just to size, overnight the toes had turned a nauseating purple colour that would have looked delicious in a fruit bowl but was completely out of place attached to my feet. The toes were so huge and painful that I couldn't put on ordinary shoes; open sandals were the only things that could accommodate these monstrous appendages. Walking was a real problem. Until that moment I hadn't appreciated how important toes are: they give that little forward spring that launches each step. Mine were useless and, without them, walking was clumsy and amazingly uncomfortable. After a few experiments, I found it easiest to take short stiff-legged strides that made me feel like a wind-up toy soldier.

I hadn't given it much thought beforehand but, hobbling awkwardly around the airport, balanced precariously on my heels, it seemed that the connections from Jakarta to London had been scheduled by a particularly malicious airline sprite. There were tortuously long waits at each airport, including an eight-hour stint in the transit lounge at Karachi. Anyone who has travelled by plane will no doubt know all about swelling feet. It is caused by sitting for hours in tiny cramped chairs, unable to walk or stretch out fully. After just an hour in the air my tortured toes began to swell even more. For the first leg of the journey I sat next to an American engineer on route from Sydney to Singapore. He was very chatty until, during a lull in conversation, I peeled back a sock to reveal a gruesome sight. The skin was now a deeply impressive mauve colour, it had become glossy and as tight as a drum. My sock looked like a bag full of ripe aubergines. This revelation completely killed all social chit-chat; the engineer shifted over to the far side of his seat and spent the rest of the trip balanced on one buttock, leaning on the window watching the South China Sea with an unnatural dedication. He was obviously convinced that his fellow passenger was carrying some hideous tropical disease and was not willing to take any chances that it might be contagious.

From start to finish the trip took twenty-seven hours. During the whole journey I knew that, sooner or later, some heavily laden traveller would stamp on my wounded toes while navigating the narrow aisle. But it didn't happen. Incredibly my feet survived unscathed and I arrived in London with plenty of time to drive to Cambridge. The necessary equipment for my talk, slides and a respectable set of clothes, were stashed in the boot of my car at the airport. It was a short drive to Cambridge, where I knew there would be somewhere to shower and change before the lecture. I arrived at the famous old college, to be greeted by the porter.

'Ah, yes Mr Leach, we've been expecting you. Would you like to freshen up before you look at the lecture theatre and join the committee for supper?' He showed me to the guests' room and arranged to collect me in half an hour. I took a quick shower and started to change into more formal clothes. After the rain forests of Borneo, this was an alien world and I was really appreciating the novelty until it was time to put on my tidy, black polished shoes. By now my toes were so distended that it was completely impossible to stuff them even half way in. All attempts to squeeze and cajole them further produced jolts of agony firing through my foot. There was no way that those travesties of feet would fit into my ordinary shoes, but I couldn't possibly present a lecture, particularly one as important as this, in bare feet.

I telephoned the porter,

'Are there any shops open around here at this time of night?'

'Certainly Sir,' he confided; 'if you'll just tell me what you would like, I'll arrange for someone to collect it.'

'Well, I really need a pair of shoes' I admitted.

'Shoes.' Porters are polite and helpful, especially to invited lecturers, but this veteran managed to convey, in a single syllable, a wealth of opinion and scorn without saying anything remotely disrespectful. Speakers were obviously expected to bring shoes with them, not to rush out at the last moment to buy a new pair.

'I'm sorry Sir, all of the shoe shops closed an hour ago. There is, however, a supermarket in the next street and I do believe it stocks footwear.'

I had no choice. After telling the porter that I didn't require supper, in open-toed sandals, I hobbled to the huge hypermarket around the corner. Even the sandals were now feeling uncomfortably tight; my toes throbbed mercilessly and progress was arthritically slow. The shop was the size of a small village and, following some unknown but inevitable natural law, the footwear department was at the furthest possible point from the door. It took some time to limp painfully through the maze of deodorants, washing powders and babies' nappies but eventually I was rewarded by the heart-warming sight of a display of shoeboxes that filled most of the back wall. But it was a cruel trick. With a sinking heart I saw that, despite their massive stock, the hypermarket only sold green wellington boots, carpet slippers and a truly staggering variety of white training shoes.

This was no time for sartorial considerations. Boots and slippers were completely out, so it had to be the white trainers. Normally I take size nine shoes, but my elephantine toes needed a lot more room than usual. Size ten was impossibly tight, the unwieldy flesh could just about be forced into size eleven but walking was out of the question. I finally bought a pair of size twelve trainers. They were snow-white with bright red stars on each heel. It was like wearing rowing boats; there was enough room around the heels for two more feet but, for the moment, my ultra-sensitive toes were comfortable and nothing else really mattered.

I walked back to the college in sandals and just before going in changed into the new trainers. The lecture theatre was at the end of a long and empty corridor which I waddled along in gargantuan shoes that made me feel like a penguin. *Slap, slap, slap, slap…* the sound of each footfall bounced off the walls and ceiling. Each stride must have been clearly heard by everyone in the entire building and probably even further afield. A frogman in flippers couldn't have made more noise. There was a short

157

flight of stairs at the end of the corridor and these were the final straw. The first two steps were easy and overconfidence crept in; over the years I had understandably grown used to the size of my feet, but now had to cope with walking mechanics on a different scale. On the third step the end of my shoe made contact with the carpet, but the ball of my foot was so far back that it completely missed the step. Instead of going up I skidded back down the steps with a resounding crunch.

A dazzling pain surged through my feet and just at that moment the door of the lecture theatre opened and there was the speaker's secretary who had arranged the event.

'Ah Michael, we were hoping you could have arrived a little earlier. Did you have any problems getting here?'

Rather than go into the whole sordid story I explained about being held up on the way back from Borneo.

'You've just arrived from the airport then. Excellent. That will sound very dramatic in the introduction.'

Before the talk started, there was about half an hour to set levels on the sound system and check that the projector was working properly. The lecture secretary introduced me to a well-dressed man who would help set up.

'This is George, he's an expert in such things, he'll give you a hand.'

George was obviously the professional 'greeter', his job was to make me feel relaxed and he did this by asking questions.

'I hear you had a few problems getting here.' He was a skilled interrogator; under his gently probing questions I related the saga of the last seventy-two hours as we checked the equipment. Fortunately the hall was still empty so my absurd feet were not yet on show.

Ten minutes before the talk was due to start, the doors were opened and I took up my position behind the lectern. The Chairman stood to welcome the audience and finished by adding,

'As you know, it is our tradition to invite a guest to present the opening remarks, and this evening we are delighted to welcome Sir George Drummond to introduce tonight's speaker.'

George stood to a wave of applause. Over the next five minutes he proceeded to describe in uncomfortably sensational and melodramatic terms my trip from Indonesia.

'Two days ago he was trapped in a tiny village in central Borneo; since then he has braved earthquakes, walked alone through swamps and hitched a lift in a canoe just to be here with you tonight.'

I was mesmerised. For the first time in my life I realised just how a series of facts can be rearranged, without telling a single untruth, to tell a story that has nothing whatsoever to do with reality. The earthquake was merely a distant rumble, the lonely walk through swamps wouldn't have challenged a Sunday afternoon hiker and the lift on the water boat was almost like catching a bus. I couldn't help wondering if this was the prosaic background to all travel stories.

The lecture went well. I could have read the telephone directory after that glowing introduction. At the end there were a few questions and then Sir George stood to give the vote of thanks. Until that moment I had been hidden behind the solid old lectern and my feet were safely protected from public view. As George finished his thanks he held out his hand, obviously inviting me to shake it. For a moment I forgot myself and stepped out onto the stage; the hall was silent until the enormous trainers began to beat and echo on the wooden floor. The slapping noise was picked up by the microphone and amplified to the furthest corners of the hall. To a man, the entire audience looked down at my ludicrous feet and gave out an audible gasp.

The embarrassment was physically painful; it really did hurt. I just couldn't take it and my own eyes dropped and, with horror, saw that the front half of each boat-like white trainer had turned brilliant scarlet. They were soaked in blood. My slight fall on the steps must have split the already over-stretched plaster strips and the wounds had reopened. Free of all restraint the swollen toes must have gone off like geysers, and judging by the evidence they had been bleeding for the whole lecture. The silence was overwhelming. I wanted the stage to open up and swallow me. After what seemed to be several hours, but was probably just a few seconds, Sir George glared at the audience and said with great passion,

'Who can imagine the terrible ordeals Michael has endured in the past few weeks? Knowing him the way I do, I am sure that he will never reveal the precise details of his agony, but we see for ourselves how much he has suffered. We are indeed grateful for his lecture this evening and wish him a speedy recovery.'

His impromptu and totally misleading speech triggered an applause that was polite at first but quickly rose to an overpowering crescendo and, before it died, several people were on their feet and clapping wildly. Luckily by then Sir George was escorting me off the stage, leaving the audience to stare in awe and admiration.

I really should have told him there and then that this wound wasn't the result of an attack by a murderous clouded leopard or maddened, charging water buffalo. But his stirring eulogy had rescued me from an impossibly humiliating position; it would have been very ungracious – and probably unwise – to admit that the injury was self-inflicted, particularly as it took place in the giant bath tub of a luxury suite in a five star hotel. Later, in the quiet of a far less flamboyant Cambridge hotel, I was forced to concede that the audience's response to the story had been intoxicating and, although I didn't appreciate it at the time, highly addictive. Nodding off to sleep that night I was struck by the irresistible thought that adventure travelling could easily become a way of life.